Think
Feel
Do

A Wellbeing Handbook for Early Years Staff

By June O'Sullivan
and Lala Manners

Welcome

This handbook suggests how we can use the nursery environment and the activities of an average nursery day to strengthen the ten elements of wellbeing we have chosen to focus on. It is a resource for staff and designed to help them think about how 'being well to do well' can work in their nursery or relevant setting. Each chapter follows the same structure for ease of use.

June O'Sullivan
An inspiring speaker, author and regular media commentator and Government advisor for Early Years, Social Business and Child Poverty, June has been instrumental in achieving a major strategic, pedagogical and cultural shift for the award winning London Early Years Foundation, resulting in an increased profile, new childcare model and stronger social impact over the past ten years.

Lala Manners
Lala Manners PhD is known in the UK and internationally as a committed educator, teacher, writer, researcher and consultant on Early Years movement development and physical activity. She has designed and delivered a range of training opportunities for a variety of professional disciplines and advocated for children's physical activity through a range of media outlets.

With grateful thanks to: Nausheen Khan, Manager LEYF Earls Court Nursery; Pauline Emmins, Manager LEYF Ford Road Nursery; Emma Miller, Manager LEYF Bushy Tails Nursery.

Photos: © Isabelle Johnson/London Early Years Foundation

Contents

Introduction

Working with young children can be both joyful and stressful. It places a lot of physical and emotional demands on staff, who spend much of the day nurturing the wellbeing of children and supporting their personal, social, emotional, physical and cognitive skills. The role also requires staff to consider the needs of parents, colleagues and any particular challenges of the local community.

Research from sector organisations such as the Early Years Alliance have found that the wellbeing of staff is a real concern and recommendations include asking employers to consider more ways to support their staff health and wellbeing.

During the pandemic, many of us experienced fear and fatigue as well as wonderful instances of deep kindness, love and support from our families, friends, colleagues and communities. As we slowly emerge from this challenging time, we must ensure that wellbeing is more than just a random selection of occasional treats and activities. It should be the guiding principle for all organisations and sit at the very heart of policy and practice.

Wellbeing is a term used by many different fields, including finance, economics, ecology and digital technology, but, for our purposes, it is highly personal – rooted in and nurtured by childhood and life experience, culture and environment. Wellbeing really frames the critical interplay between mind and body; it underpins and informs how you feel about your place in the world, what freedoms you enjoy or would like to have, your attitude to work and downtime, how you navigate relationships, what remedies you turn to when unwell and your approach to personal grooming and maintenance.

How we cope when 'stuff happens' is also unique to each of us; do you: phone your mum or a friend – put the kettle on – go for a run or swim – pray – water your plants – have a hot bath – eat chocolate?! For some people though, negative experiences of discrimination, financial concerns and relationship issues seriously affect their daily lives – so developing wellbeing strategies that can mitigate the impact of these experiences is essential.

There is no 'quick fix' or 'one size fits all' when it comes to wellbeing – but it is vital that everyone understands what it means for them, to find ways to look after themselves and to really value what they do and who they are.

Wellbeing is for the here and now – not just for days off and holidays!

Wellbeing in the workplace is a hot topic – and rightly so. Many consider that a supportive, open-minded organisational culture is critical for it to be properly addressed. Such a culture means staff feel more comfortable about including their personal and private selves in their professional lives, and equality of wellbeing in all three domains then becomes a lived reality. Through communicating, listening and trusting others – we can ensure that self-care is not considered selfish but an essential part of daily life.

Chapter 1

The Power of Body Image

What do we know about body image?

Bodies have always been shaped by cultural moments and practices. Each era has its own unique and recognisable 'identifying markers' that can tell us immediately which historical period people fit into.

So, what are our 'identifying markers' and how do they impact on the way we value, nurture and manage our physical selves today?

In many ways, our bodies are no longer just 'things to be washed, deodorised, dressed and perfumed' before getting on with the day. Sadly, for some of us, they have become a source of anxiety, discontent, anger and abuse.

The daily messages we receive about our bodies – especially via celebrity media platforms – can be overwhelming. They portray a standard of beauty that is completely unrealistic and dependent on products and interventions that high-profile individuals are often paid to promote. But do these people ever admit to using Botox or fillers unless caught out? Think of the outcry when an unfiltered celebrity photo is published – it is very revealing!

Did you know that the total advertising budget spent on social influencers for beauty products in the US and the UK will rise from $5bn in 2019 to $10bn in the next five years. Interestingly, this will impact on all genders, colours, cultures and ages, but we do know that younger people respond more positively to aggressive marketing. So, question everything and always ask who profits from believing these messages? And do they make me feel better or worse about myself?

A certain amount of body anxiety is perfectly normal. Drs Lindsay and Lexie Kite, authors of 'More Than A Body', say that feeling uncomfortable about our bodies is entirely natural. We all have bits we like and bits we don't and wish could be different. We tend to use humour to manage our body issues and to cover up any obvious body envy, but this doesn't really support a positive and healthy relationship with our bodies that is our primary aim here.

Advertising really doesn't help, as it is based on two fundamental beliefs:

1. that health and happiness depend on appearance;

2. that you are only worthy of health and happiness if you buy into the right products and services.

"A certain amount of body anxiety is perfectly normal."

Drs Lindsay and Lexie Kite, authors of 'More Than A Body'

Young men can also experience body anxiety, but often face the 'masculinity barrier' and find it difficult to talk about their body issues, emotions, anxiety or unhappiness. Their coping strategies (like many of us) can often be solitary and unhealthy – and their support mechanisms unreliable and questionable.

Remember, 'comparison is the thief of joy'. Constantly comparing yourself to others can make you feel defeated and miserable, and is a complete waste of time and energy!

Many staff working in Early Years are in their forties and fifties, which means they will experience the menopause. Although this is a natural process, it is often a taboo subject even though all women will go through it at some point in their lives – there are no celebrity exemptions!

Approximately 34 symptoms are associated with the menopause that can affect our bodies and minds – everything from poor memory and concentration, hot flushes, weight gain to anxiety and difficulty sleeping. Read Caroline Vollans' excellent book called 'Menopause' – a series of interviews with 35 women from a wide range of cultures and backgrounds that explores their responses to the menopause.

Ultimately, our bodies should be 'a reliable place to live from' – and work as well as possible for us – so that valuable time and energy is not taken up constantly agitating about them. Our era's 'identifying markers' around bodies include the obsession with physical perfection – acute body anxiety – disordered eating, the rise of social media platforms, use of digital enhancement, Instagram feeds, TikTok, blogs, vlogs and dubious surgical interventions. Are we sure we want to be remembered for all this?

Fit and healthy bodies come in all different shapes and sizes, and the roads to a happy body are many, varied and wide enough for everyone. We need to trust that our bodies will work competently and efficiently so we can get on with the business of living!

Remember, our bodies are primarily wonderfully effective instruments, not just ornaments to be decorated and admired.

ABOUT **YOU**

Two Fun Activities about YOU – that you can do by yourself or in a group.

'I AM': You will need: a piece of A4 paper, a selection of magazines, glue, scissors, felt tips/crayons.

What to do: Draw a big 'I AM' in the middle of the page. Take your time and begin to cut out any words from the magazines you feel best describe you personally. Stick them on the page in any pattern. Discuss with friends and colleagues as you go – you may be surprised at some of your choices!

. . . .

Describe ... This is always an interesting one to do in a small group and highlights how many of us are strangely uncomfortable about accepting compliments and being positive about ourselves.

What to do: You will need pen and paper to write down all the things you most like/admire and appreciate about someone who is very close to you. Now write your name with the letters going downwards and against each letter write something that best describes YOU, beginning with each letter of your name. Discuss this with your group.

What do we notice about children's body image?

Children tend to take their bodies for granted – unless and until something goes wrong, they hurt themselves or become ill in some way. What they really want to do is move as much as possible, continually practising their physical skills and collaborating with their peers to create increasingly challenging and interesting movement opportunities.

Most children are perfectly comfortable in and about their bodies. Although they are vaguely interested when their teeth fall out, they need new shoes, or they can miraculously swim and ride a bike, fussing about what they look like or what other people think of them is not usually a significant part of their daily lives.

There are many factors that influence how they see themselves and, as adults, we can play a critical role in helping them develop a positive body image and good self-esteem.

It's difficult for anyone to escape the 'ideal' body image that is promoted by today's media – either in print or on screen. Children are definitely not immune to these messages that can very subtly seep through to them in the way we move, in our body language and what we talk about when we think they aren't listening!

Frowning if we can't do up a zip – groaning when we get up off the floor – looking longingly at a lunchtime potato – being continually self-deprecating about our physical appearance and competence – labelling very physically able children 'heedless', 'wild' or 'reckless', can all impact on how children see their own physical skills and abilities being valued and supported. They will pick up immediately on any negative body messages and will repeat, embellish

and remember any mention of diets, weight and scales that can be mighty difficult to erase.

We need to ensure that none of the following beliefs take root in their lives. It is definitely worth thinking about these statements and seeing if any apply to you – they relate to both women and men.

The big question to ask of each point is WHY may I think like this?
• My body has to be perfect.
• I'm not satisfied with my body.
• A perfect body would make me happy.
• A perfect body would earn me acceptance from others.
• A perfect body would earn love and admiration, even attention.
• Perfection is defined by a number on the scale or a size on a tag.
• I will do anything to have a perfect body.

In working with children, we have a brilliant opportunity to move more and sit less – but we need to learn how to enjoy doing this and not find it a chore. We should recognise that, like children, our mental and emotional wellbeing is closely linked to our physical selves, our confidence, competence and general health.

Children's physical and mental health work together, in a continual two-way flow. When they can move freely in a safe and supportive environment, with lots of interesting resources to explore – if they can initiate play, join in, keep up and contribute then a lot falls into place for them. Their emotional equilibrium is very dependent on physical competence and confidence – what they can do physically matters way more to them than literacy and numeracy. But, as we know, reading emerges from spoken language and where does this mostly happen … during physical play!

Watch your babies, infants and children move whenever and wherever possible. Notice how they have an urge to 'fidget'. What positions they choose to sit in and how often they change them. One-year-olds will change position about every two minutes if left alone to do so.

Sadly, many of the 'incidental' opportunities to move throughout the day have disappeared from children's lives. We know in the last ten years babies have lost approx. 600 hours' tummy time in their first year – and the 'roaming distance' for older children has decreased from three miles to 300 yards in a generation. This has much to do with changes in lifestyle, screentime, modern parenting styles and changes to the curriculum.

Children's ability to test their physical competence and enjoy using their bodies to learn can be compromised if we are always telling them to 'stop', 'be careful', 'hold on', 'we don't do that here' You may think these warnings are essential, but they need to push a few boundaries, find out what they can do, especially those very physically energetic children who quickly become disheartened by negative reactions to their ideas.

'Swooping and scooping' – when you rush to the rescue every time – also doesn't support their confidence to manage their bodies independently. It's always done with the best of intentions, but stop and think if it's really necessary and what the learning opportunities may be in allowing the outcome to unfold naturally.

There is much talk at the moment about self-regulation, the ways in which children learn to understand and manage their emotions and their individual ways of learning. Physical activity and movement play are the ideal ways for children to begin to recognise, regulate and manage their emotional lives safely and securely.

What message will we champion at work?

Children use their whole bodies to learn and therefore we need to be just as comfortable with how we use our own bodies to model their learning. If our bodies are exhausted, in pain, or under daily stress, this will affect our emotional state and professional ability. An approach to wellbeing that is rooted in, and nourished by, our practice is now essential.

We are actually in a strong position to begin with, as most of us in the Early Years have daily access to some form of outside space, fresh air, healthy food and enjoy the company of colleagues and children. Let's try to be more childlike, by moving and appreciating each other's positive energy through being active together.

Read children's classic books like 'Giraffes Can't Dance' by Giles Andreae and Guy Parker-Rees, sing with Eric Carle's 'Head to Toes' or take a walk with 'I Went Walking' by Sue Williams.

Include movement play in their daily routine inside and outdoors – and in all weathers! Also make sure it is properly represented in daily planning and not just slotted in as a scheduled activity a few times a week.

Check out useful websites for children/ movement such as www.activematters.org or www.earlymovers.org and www.beinspireduk.co.uk

Self-care is also an important aspect of children's physicality and growing independence, so our choice of nursery activities and resources to support this really matters. Carefully preparing the doctor's role play area can open up conversations about how their bodies work and need to be looked after.

Other nursery activities that are really good for encouraging a positive body image include children painting themselves while looking in a mirror, celebrating their hair during hairdressing role play, accessing resources that are representative of them, and choosing books that focus on body positivity across all generations and cultures.

Be aware of gender issues around children's clothes and resources

Do girls need to be in pink and boys in blue? Not according to the pink stinks campaign! www.pinkstinks.co.uk. It's very useful to be reminded again that what we say and do around children's bodies has a real impact on their developing beliefs.

Thoughts for today, and every day!

- My body is strong and healthy and does what I want it to do
- I am proud of what my body does for me
- I will value and respect my body in ways that work for me
- I will accept and embrace the way my body changes over time
- I am my own kind of beautiful
- Cut out negative self-talk. Be realistic!

Bitesize help

Read: 'Women Don't Owe You Pretty' and 'More Than a Body' by Drs Lindsay and Lexie Kite

Listen: www.ted.com/talks/felicity_hayward_the_great_body_positivity_swindle

Watch: www.jamessmithacademy.com

Check out: www.morethanabody.org and www.time-to-change.org.uk

Start a journal

Journaling just means setting aside a little quiet, undistracted time to sit down and think about your life. It may include writing down a record of what happened that day, offloading about something that is really bothering you or noting something that has inspired you.

Chapter 2

Moving is Soothing

What do we know about movement?

The relationship between movement and overall health goes back a very long way. The ancient disciplines of Yoga and Tai Chi have at their heart a very close link between movement and emotional wellbeing and there is growing recognition in the therapeutic world that because rhythm and regulation are closely linked then engaging in calming, repetitive, rhythmic movements will have a beneficial effect on mood and behaviours.

Medical writers as far back as the second century writer Juvenal, wrote that a sound/rational mind in a healthy body is something to proactively maintain. The eighteenth-century Scottish doctor William Buchan strongly believed that 'the want of proper exercise made people's lives short and miserable.'

The terms 'movement' and 'exercise' tend to be used interchangeably, but are subtly different.
Most of us can move a bit every day (some more than others) – it is difficult to avoid moving at all. Exercise is described as a 'voluntary physical activity undertaken for the sake of fitness' and many people manage to avoid it completely!

In a 2015 report by the USA Academy of Medical Royal College, exercise was described as a 'wonder drug' and 'miracle cure' because the benefits were so great for so little outlay. The report suggests that movement provides 'order for the body because it helps organise the body to stay healthy and functional' and exercise is a chance to 'educate our bodies and minds at once so the body supports the brain's ability to function and operate effectively'.

Let's take a closer look at what the evidence says about the benefits of moving and exercising.

What does moving/exercising do for us physically?

- Blood flow is increased that leads to better circulation, digestion and heart and lung function
- Neurogenesis in the brain is increased and promoted – when moving our brains produce new cells that improve memory and performance
- Blood pressure is reduced
- Sugar levels are balanced out
- Upper body strength and hand grip are increased
- Lower back pain is alleviated
- Osteoarthritis in the knee is alleviated
- Flow in the lymphatic system is increased; this body system has no pump of its own so relies on movement to function well – it is responsible for removing unwanted debris so our bodies are better able to fight infection and viruses
- Cholesterol level is decreased
- Exercise is known to reduce the risk of dementia, heart disease and some cancers by 30%
- It helps support the efficiency of insulin metabolism and reduces the risk of Type 2 Diabetes
- It provides 'order' for the body – it helps the body stay healthy and functional

What moving/exercise can do for us mentally?

- Moving can strengthen the hippocampus in the brain, an area that plays a major role in learning and memory and is known to decrease in volume in people with dementia and depression
- The sympathetic nervous system is calmed and synchronised; this regulates the 'arousal' or fight/flight response to stress
- Anxiety and depression are reduced due to increased blood flow to the brain
- Production of the mood-enhancing hormone dopamine is increased
- Production of the neurotransmitter serotonin and 'feel-good' endorphins are triggered
- The protein BDNF (brain-derived neurotropic factor) is stimulated and protects existing brain cells and promotes new, healthier cells, leading to better brain function
- Stress levels and cortisol production are lowered
- Touch releases oxytocin – the 'calm and connected' hormone
- Self-image and body confidence is improved, leading to fewer self-critical moments

What happens if we don't move!

This is actually a very modern problem! No one in the Stone Age went for a five-mile jog to stave off decrepitude or lifted weights whose sole purpose was to be lifted. Instead, humans moved to survive as they hunted, fished and built settlements. They also moved for pleasure as they danced, celebrated and enjoyed social rituals.

Astronauts, who live in a weightless environment for extended periods, do practically no muscle work and the results are dramatic. They can lose up to 20 per cent of their muscle mass in ten days, 1.5 per cent of bone mass per month (60 X the normal rate of aging) and after four months this will take two years to regain. This tells us that we are not like jellyfish wafting aimlessly along ocean currents but that we have evolved to be physically active and our bones and muscles need continual stimulation to do the job they were designed for.

It is also worth remembering that after a month of lying in bed, inactive muscles lose 50% of their strength, ligaments lose 60% of their function and tendons become less useful. So, it is essential we keep moving so we can prevent accidents and ensure we don't end up in bed for prolonged periods!

How much movement do we really need?
The experts say we should aim to do 2.5 hours or 150 minutes moderate exercise (walking, gardening, cycling, swimming and household chores) or 75 minutes vigorous exercise (sprinting, weights, rowing) per week. Around 30 per cent of adults currently do less than 30 minutes per week! But we can all start somewhere and this involves moving daily, gently and consistently so your body gets used to being more active – and you begin to enjoy and feel the benefits.

Weaving together our personal wellbeing needs and professional roles starts with what we do with the children every day. Often, our wellbeing needs get squeezed into any free time after work but instead, we need to think how we can best benefit from the activities we do with the children and maximise the opportunities we have to move and be active throughout the working day.

Dr Tim Spector wrote in his very accessible book, 'Spoon Fed', that exercise should be 'the number one prescribed drug'. His simple recommendations include: move a bit every 15 minutes or so, if only to wriggle or stretch; potter around a lot; use the stairs whenever possible; and keep gently active throughout the day. Include frequent bouts of fairly energetic movement and sometimes zoom around and get properly puffed.

This is an average day in the nursery! Try to join in some of the children's movement activities. Everyday tasks like setting the table, washing the chairs, scrubbing the dollies or tidying up indoors are really useful ways to keep our joints mobilised and core muscles strong through bending and stretching. Running jumping, climbing, digging and constructing outside with children can also get us nicely puffed and energised! Remember, when we move, we soothe our heads, our sore bodies and our busy brains; we laugh, we bond; we breathe and we feel more positive about our lives.

Fact Flash

Moving for just eight minutes a day or about one hour a week can make a significant difference to overall health and wellbeing.

Movement really is a child's first language

What do we notice about how children move?

Physical activity and movement play are essential for ensuring that children's overall development is smooth and harmonious.

From birth onwards, they learn about themselves and their environment through continual practice and refinement of physical skills.

As they become more confident and competent physically, they begin to navigate their surroundings with ease and determine their own risks and challenges.

Movement really is their first language, the floor their first playground, and the primary way in which they begin to understand themselves and their place in the world.

Children's emotional and mental wellbeing is intrinsically connected to how they are doing physically. We notice quite quickly when their equilibrium is affected by being in pain, too tired, hungry, wet, hot or cold. We may see tears, tantrums, withdrawal, aggression or a need for hugs and cuddles.

For us and for children, this links closely to the interoceptive sense – often called the 'hidden eighth sense'. Interoception is hugely important in that it tells us what is going on inside our bodies, for example when we feel full, tired, sick, sleepy or thirsty. The beautifully named 'Island of Rhial', in the insular cortex of the brain, helps coordinate essential information from internal organs and the skin.

Children gain a good interoceptive sense through lots of movement play and being physically active. So, for example, there is a strong link between tummy time for babies when the soft tissue around the

Movement is also often called the 'currency' of childhood because of the high value children themselves place on physical skills. Being physically active is how friendships are created and sustained, how disputes are settled and how children from different backgrounds and cultures can share experiences. You may remember playing Stone, Scissors, Paper or Cat's Cradle, the Fruit Salad Running Game, Bulldog, High Low Chika Low and joining in clapping games or French skipping when friendships were immediately formed and enjoyed.

middle is being stimulated and, later on, time continence when children need to know when to go. The link between bodily sensations and emotions is crucial, because the consequences of getting the wrong message can be significant. Children need to know if they are really hungry or actually just thirsty, if they are tired or simply need an energy boost, and how comfortable they feel around certain people. This is what 'listening to' or 'tuning into' your body really means. It supports children (and us) to answer the question 'How do you feel?' with knowledge and confidence.

We also know that the most physically competent and confident children have the most mature social skills, a wider circle of friends and a more extensive vocabulary. New vocabulary may be acquired in a relevant and meaningful context as children experience being active together. This is especially important for children learning two languages or struggling with their communication skills who really thrive on the parity of status afforded them in movement play. It provides the optimum environment for all children to gain and maintain trust in themselves, adults and friends.

It is recommended that all young children should be physically active for 180 minutes over an average a day. This works out at around 25% of their waking time, so in a three-hour session, they should be moving for at least 45 minutes. If you make arriving and leaving more active, create active circle times and allow for an extended outdoor play session, 45 minutes is quite achievable. Children's bodies need to move little and often and, for older children, a good 60 minutes of properly vigorous play every day is recommended. Much like us, they need continual recalibration to be comfortable. Left to their own devices, they will rarely sit cross-legged (it is so uncomfortable!) and happily change position every few minutes because pressure on the spinal discs increases by 30% after ten minutes' sitting still!

Lullabies, soothing songs and rocking together is calming for children, and adults, as heartbeats and movements are synchronised. But remember that being energetic together (holding hands and jumping, running, making a circle and moving in and out and dancing to music) can be equally bonding and comforting.

What can we champion at work?

We need to be happy movers ourselves, so we can encourage more movement in our nurseries. You can do the following exercises at any point of the day when you need a moment or feel overwhelmed. Try each option and choose those that work best for you.

4 breathing exercises
These are best done sitting comfortably.

1 Box breathing

Inhale for the count of four. Hold your breath in for the count of four. Breathe out for the count of four. Hold your breath out for the count of four. You can increase the count to five, six or eight when you feel comfortable to do so. Try to do this for one minute at a time, slowly reducing your breaths from 12–20bpm – to around 6.

2 Nose breathing

Using your right hand, place your thumb and ring finger over both nostrils. Lift your thumb away from your right nostril and breathe in for the count of four. Close both nostrils for the count of four and hold the breath in. Now lift your ring finger to breathe out for a count of four. Repeat as often as you like.

3 Blowing candles

Line your right forefinger up with your nose, about 20–40cms away at eye level. Imagine this finger is a candle and start to blow very softly to make it flicker. Take long, slow breaths in and out.

4 Cushion breathing

On the floor, lie on your back with knees bent and feet on the floor. Place a small cushion on your tummy, keep your arms long by your sides. Now breathe in for a count of six and out for a count of six. Notice the cushion rise and fall as you breathe.

where they are and how to deal with them!

Jaw: Many people clench their teeth tightly either overnight or for extended periods in the day. Therefore, every so often, open your mouth wide, puff out your cheeks, try to yawn and gently massage the tense areas whenever possible.

Neck: This comes from daily demands – often from tucking mobiles under chins and trying to do other jobs at the same time! Always put mobiles on loudspeaker. Gently ease out your neck at every possible opportunity, especially after carrying children/shopping.

Shoulders: Affected throughout the day, often from gripping handles of buggies or steering wheels very tightly, carrying shoulders too high when tired/anxious, not moving the joints often enough. A simple action is to roll up a tea towel into a snake shape. Hold either end and, with long arms, slowly pull the material from thigh level to high above your head. Have a good wiggle, bend and straighten your arms. Bring it back down and repeat. Remember to frequently push buggies with open hands for a few seconds at a time – stretch and wiggle your fingers.

Backs: Also affected daily by general demands – often from carrying children on one hip and poor bedding. Answer: Use a wall to massage the back. Face a wall and place your hands on the wall at shoulder height. Take a step back, gently move hips side to side/backwards and forwards and breathe. Now turn around and press your shoulders only against the wall. Rock from one shoulder to the other. Now press your bottom only against the wall and rock from one side to the other. Finally, put your hands on your knees, drop your head towards your chest and breathe. Also remember that the shock-absorbing discs in the spine are 80% water, so keep hydrated!

- Think about finding ways to move gently and consistently throughout the day. Make sure whatever you do is manageable, accessible and sustainable.

- Tune into' and 'listen to' your body. How is your breathing? Are you particularly tense anywhere? And are there any sore places to deal with?

- Create a 'bank' of calming options that work for you and recognise any habits you have got into that may not really be helping, e.g. pacing, squeezing thumbs, pushing fists into palms.

- Think about your reactions to being physically active. Once you are used to moving more, you can begin to explore exercise options that may suit you and your body.

Start a journal

Journaling just means setting aside a little quiet, undistracted time to sit down and think about your life. It may include writing down a record of what happened that day, offloading about something that is really bothering you or noting something that has inspired you.

Thoughts for today, and every day!

Never forget the power of the lullaby. Sing along with Dorothy in the Wizard of Oz.

"Somewhere over the rainbow, way up high
There's a land that I heard of once in a lullaby
Somewhere over the rainbow, skies are blue
And the dreams that you dare to dream
Really do come true ..."

Bitesize help

Read: 'MOVE!' Caroline Williams, Profile Books 2021

Watch: www.headspace.com/bbc

Listen: Relaxing music and sounds

Check Out: www.futurelearn.com/courses/supporting-physical-development-early-childhood

www.playmoveimprove.com.au/collections/free-downloads/products/free-classroom-gross-motor-skills-week-lesson-plan-printable

Chapter 3

The Pleasure of Small Things

What do we know about small pleasures?

For many of us, 2020 was the year in which we properly connected with our local communities – when we really understood the value of our immediate environment – when we more fully appreciated local shops and services and noticed the interesting, quirky, strange, unusual, challenging features of our neighbourhoods.

The rhythm of our days changed – and often became slower, quieter and more reflective; we could sometimes hear early-morning birdsong and even found the quiet humming chatter on our commutes less intrusive. We began to appreciate what Thomas Weaver (2015) describes as 'the poetry of the back garden'.

We learned in the past year how valuable communities are – that isolation is not good for us long-term and that we need to experience a range of daily interactions to keep us ticking over. Not all communication had to be deep and meaningful; waving to the postman, saying hello to the local shopkeeper, calling to the elderly as we walked past their homes, smiling at children still going to school all mattered just as much as the extended Zoom sessions with work colleagues, the necessary family call and the walk in a park with a friend. We learned to look out for those who were vulnerable and struggling.

As Professor Bruce Perry says, 'being human doesn't necessarily make us humane' – but we were offered the perfect opportunity to give it our best shot.

"Being human doesn't necessarily make us humane"
Professor Bruce Perry

Isolation and loneliness

Isolation and loneliness emerged as a latent and significant problem. Over nine million people in the UK, one fifth of the population, say they are always or often lonely and over one million of our elderly speak to no one from one month to the next. We know this situation is deeply harmful to our health and that lacking social connections is as much a risk factor for early death as smoking 15 cigarettes a day. Loneliness also increases the likelihood of mortality by 26 per cent, so it is not surprising that most wellbeing initiatives include 'communication' as one of their central principles.

9m

Over nine million people in the UK suffer from loneliness

The Early Years sector is in a unique position to help, because we are usually situated at the very heart of local communities and communication on every level is part and parcel of our everyday lives. We can nurture close relationships whose roots are deep and sustainable, we can support local enterprises, use local amenities and connect the generations between 0 to 90-plus years. LEYF is among many organisations that believe that nurseries should act as 'community catalysts – to stimulate engagement between people who live and work near each other.

'Belonging' is a concept that forms a very strong thread through the LEYF pedagogy and is closely linked to children's emerging identity that is informed by a respectful and close relationship with their environment.

'Belonging' also has another component that relates to everything we have explored so far about body image and care. For all of us (children included), it means having a calm and peaceful relationship with your body – an affinity with yourself that is deeply personal and meaningful. 'Belonging' means being happy in your body – a body that is completely at home in the environment and community in which you work and live. The author Brené Brown says that 'True belonging doesn't require that we change who we are. It requires us to be who we are.'

Fact Flash

Loneliness and isolation can be found everywhere, in every age group and from every background, but in our own small world, we can open our doors to the community, create opportunities to build deep and meaningful connections, form networks and build strong bridges between people.'

Multigenerational activities are a great way of fostering children's sense of belonging

What do we notice about how children experience pleasure?

Children are observers. They notice and are intrigued by small things; cats sitting in windows, weeds growing in the pavement, railings to peek through, shop windows to investigate, passing buses, sirens, steps to climb, walls to balance on, puddles to stamp in, a digger laying cables, dustbins being collected ...

They also really like doing the same thing again and again; going for the same walk to see if the same tree is still there, if the pile of builder's sand remains, if the bulbs have emerged or the scaffolding is still there. Small changes in seasons and weather are also important as they impact on choices of clothing, food and opportunities to socialise.

Physically, they are always extraordinarily interested in small body parts; eyebrows and lashes, nostrils, ear lobes, tummy buttons, fingernails, and will endlessly explore and compare.

Children like company and they enjoy feeling part of the community. The activities they missed most included visiting parks and shops, the library, cafes and other local amenities. They also really missed their friends and many parents commented they had not realised quite how much friendships mattered to their children at this young age.

Multigenerational activities are a great way of fostering children's sense of belonging in the community, especially when it also involves their parents. For example, when a LEYF community member initiates an activity across all the nurseries like 'Positivity Week' – everyone is encouraged to say something positive and genuine to people they meet whether it is complimenting the administrator, thanking the milkman or sending an email to Central Office to say how much their support is appreciated.

What message will we champion at work?

Small pleasures are exactly that, small but effective; a warm welcome in the morning, a big smile, saying thank you, a compliment well-meant or finding a fun mug for a new staff member to say 'hello.' Regular treats are also welcome like asking the chef to lay out a cooked breakfast especially on a cold morning or having a little sweet treat on a Friday in the staff room. You can plan more 'get-together days', spend a little more reflective time with your colleagues and organise a few regular fun events, like bowling, the cinema or a meal out together.

At break time, encourage staff to chat and get to know each other a little better. This really helps you to spot if something is not quite right, to find the best moment to gently ask if everything is OK and if they feel like talking sometime. If you are the manager, make sure the office has an open door.

Small communications for children are also vital, a reassuring smile from the other side of the room, a little tap on the shoulder or squeeze – all say, in a simple way, 'I'm thinking of you; you are in my mind.'

Invite children to explore and collect a range of small things inside and outdoors to put into very small containers such as mini jam jars, Tic Tac boxes, travel-sized and Kinder egg containers and travel sweet tins.

Appreciate and look after your work environment. Take pleasure in placing small, nurturing touches around your nursery. Put a bowl of colourful fruit or flowers in the staff area, indulge in little 'pamper boxes' in the bathroom, send a handwritten card to your colleagues, buy or make little treats and maybe invest in a staff coffee machine!

In Frances Edmonds' book, 'Repotting your life', she suggests we look at the foundations of our lives in terms of a jar filled with rocks, pebbles and sand.

We should all try to rediscover our pleasure in small things.

We should all try to rediscover our pleasure in small things. If we don't pay attention to small things or notice how they make us think and feel, we won't ever find the real joy they can bring. If we're always fixated on the next big thing looming on the horizon, we will forget to properly enjoy what the present has to offer.

Rocks go in first. These represent the fundamental things in your life that you absolutely cannot live without. They will be very personal and may change as you age, or in response to events. Rocks may include your home, family, place of worship, work, sport and nature.

Pebbles come next. These are significant to your life, but less critical. They may include your friends, hobbies and travel. Sand is poured last into the jar. This includes the fun things you like doing, things you look forward to, what you may like to do in the future, all the small things that make you laugh and make you feel good.

Try this activity either in a group or by yourself; you may be surprised ...

- On a sheet of paper, draw the outline of a jar. Draw some rocks at the bottom and write on them what they represent to you.

- Now add some pebbles and write on them what they represent – may they become rocks in the future?

- Now sprinkle in your sand. What makes up this for you? May it eventually form pebbles?

- Of course, you may also like to source a real jar, with real rocks, pebbles and sand as a reminder of your choices!

- What are your top five 'small things'?

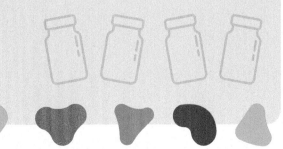

Thoughts for today, and every day!

Life is so full of frantic busyness that its often hard to appreciate how happy the small things in life can make us; the smell of ground coffee and fresh, warm bread, the sound of laughter, a beautiful sunrise, a hot bath, a good book, clean sheets, lovely music ... such tiny, seemingly insignificant things can provide so much pleasure.

Here is a snippet from Maitreyabandhu, The Crumb Road, Bloodaxe Books (2013)

There's no law against my listening
To this thrush behind the barn,
The song so loud it echoes like a bell,
Then is further off beyond the lawn.
Whatever else there is, there's this as well.

Start a journal

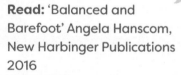

Journaling just means setting aside a little quiet, undistracted time to sit down and think about your life. It may include writing down a record of what happened that day, offloading about something that is really bothering you or noting something that has inspired you.

Bitesize help

Read: 'Balanced and Barefoot' Angela Hanscom, New Harbinger Publications 2016

Read: 'The Hidden Pleasures of Life: A New Way of Remembering the Past and Imagining the Future' by Theodore Zeldin (2016)

Watch: How Yarn Bombing Became a Worldwide Movement

Listen: To someone read 'The Boy, The Mole, The Fox and The Horse' by Charles Mackesy

Check Out: 'The Joy of Small Things' by Hannah Jane Parkinson

Chapter 4

Boundaries and Limits

What do we know about boundaries?

A boundary, according to the writer Anne Katherine, is like a membrane that keeps an organism intact. It lets positive things through. It keeps harmful things out. In this way, it operates quite differently from a defence, which indiscriminately keeps things out.

We use boundaries to keep children safe and teach them to keep safe. We create a sense of safety and boundaries by clarifying what is expected of them and then reinforcing this consistently through the routine and daily expectations of how they can behave, so that the children learn how to respond to situations and know what to do and how to behave in many circumstances.

In the wider world, creating and maintaining of personal boundaries has become an integral part of the wellbeing movement, considered essential to self-care and to ensure we are happy and functioning individuals.

Boundaries can be visible or invisible; they are intimate, emotional, spiritual, financial, material and may be linked to time, energy and environment. Some may be flexible, others non-negotiable. Whatever form they take, they are unique and important to us; they preserve our personal space, protect the 'inner core' of our identity and ensure our right to choices. They make sure we feel safe and secure, not vulnerable and exposed.

Boundaries play a pivotal role in our lives and are often linked to values, belief systems and culture. The social pedagogues among you will recognise this approach as the '3 Ps' that identify our private, personal and professional boundaries.

Private: This is really the inner core or essence of you – what makes you. It is the place where your self-actualisation, self-worth and self-esteem are incubated and nurtured, where expectations, hopes and dreams live, and which can be a fragile place at times. Probably very few people ever get to know this part of you, but if threatened in any way, this is the place where some of the non-negotiable boundaries around self-care/preservation will be found.

Personal: This is the face you like to present to the world, your 'daily face' where your attitudes, prejudices, agendas, who you befriend/value/trust and admire are to be found. Family often sit here and setting boundaries around their behaviours and agendas is very common and sometimes necessary.

Boundaries are often intrinsically linked with our childhood cultures and will frame certain behaviours, including relationships with older members of the community.

Professional: This is where issues may arise if you are expected to support or asked to do things that may not align with your personal and private lives. Managing this conflict involves making little micro-tweaks, adjustments and compromises that ensure life runs as smoothly as possible. This sphere may be the place where setting boundaries becomes a challenge to maintain and justify.

To create and maintain effective boundaries requires courage, confidence, strength and belief – but we must always be vigilant that our boundaries are beneficial and don't just become an excuse to avoid responsibilities.

Boundaries should support us to fulfil our potential, extend our experiences and help us to explore and grow.

For this to happen, we need to feel secure, strong and in control of our decisions. Ultimately, boundaries should be positive for our wellbeing and enable us to live our best lives.

Here is an exercise that you may find useful.

Carefully consider what personal rights you think you do have or should have. Here are a few ideas to get you started.

My confidence charter
I have the right to:
- be successful – and to acknowledge the success of others
- make mistakes – and learn from them in a way that works for me
- make decisions – and accept the consequences
- ask for what I want – but know the answer may sometimes be 'No'
- to have a point of view and opinions of my own
- to have feelings and emotions – and voice them appropriately
- to change my mind – and accept that other people can do the same
- privacy – and to respect the privacy of others
- change myself if I want to
- believe in myself
- ask for help – without feeling embarrassed or guilty
- be loved and to show love and give love
- take time off from household tasks and chores
- be healthy and well in ways that suit me
- have fun in ways that are appropriate and suit me.

3 helpful exercises to support your level of confidence

These three exercises will also support your level of confidence. The first is about finding your voice to say 'No'. Remember, 'No' can be a complete sentence!

1 **No, No, No, No, No, No, No, No, No, No, No, No**
1 2 3 4 5 6 7 8 9 10 11 12

Start at No 1 and say 'No' very, very quietly – almost whispering.

Gradually move from 1–12 and say 'No', getting louder each time. At what point do you start to feel uncomfortable with the volume? How do you feel when it gets to 11/12?

2 **Think of different ways to say 'No', but remain pleasant. Here are some ideas, please add your own!**

- 'Let me think about that.'
- 'Here's what will work for me.'
- 'Can I get back to you?'
- 'That doesn't really work for me.'
- 'I appreciate you asking. Sorry, but I really can't today.'
- I know this is important, but I just can't do it right now.'
- Thanks, but this isn't going to work.'
- 'That isn't possible for me right now.'
- 'Oh, I wish I could.'
- 'I can help you find a solution.'

3 **Can you think of an example in a) your personal life and b) your professional life when you have said 'No' – and meant it.**

How did you feel about it – and did it have the effect you wanted or expected?

What do we notice about children's boundaries?

When we talk about boundaries in terms of children, we are usually focusing on their behaviour. We say things like, 'I need to put up some boundaries/They don't have any boundaries at home/We need to work with them on boundaries.'

We are aiming to set limits on their behaviour so they remain safe and healthy and the development of their ability to self-regulate is supported appropriately.

But we should be aware that, like us, children can have private and personal boundaries that they may sometimes find difficult to align with behavioural expectations in the nursery.

If we think about a 'confidence charter' for children, what may it contain?

Here are a few initial ideas, please add your own.

I have the right to:
- be asked if you want something from me. please don't just take it without explaining why first
- be included in the conversation, if you are talking about me to other people and I am there
- be asked if I want to be picked up/hugged/cuddled/kissed
- be asked if I want my nose wiped/nappy changed/hair tousled
- decide if I want to join in or not with activities – if/when appropriate
- decide if I want my photograph taken – or not
- have time and space to be alone and quiet if I want to
- move and be active when I need to be
- contribute to plans that include me and to have choices if/when appropriate

Children may well bring with them cultural boundaries around touch, gender, eye contact, independence and personal responsibility; some boundaries may be unknown until a situation arises when they need to be acknowledged.

Being sensitive and respectful of children's boundaries is essential; so how can we set limits for their behaviour that do not compromise their enjoyment, keep them healthy and safe and are valid, necessary and fit for purpose?

The nursery day can be hugely demanding for young children; some are spending ten hours a day with us and experiencing a level of tiredness, noise, stimulation and emotional pressure that many of us would struggle with.

Managing themselves requires patience, practice and time. They cannot get everything right all at once and inevitably we will be faced with 'behaviour that challenges'. We must be ready and able to offer appropriate support to children who may need extra help to manage the frustrations, annoyances and irritations of an average day.

Balancing our need to set limits with the urge children have to push them is well known to teachers of all ages – not just Early Years!

Children thrive when the limits set make sense and when they do not compromise their personal and private boundaries too much. The better we know our children and understand their developmental needs, personalities, temperaments and home circumstances, the more we can align the two and minimise the possibility of conflict.

To think about:
- Routines are a really good way to help children learn what behaviours are related to specific contexts. Use visual timetables to help children.
- Be aware that projecting any personal anxieties and fears around risky and adventurous play often curtails children's need to find the limits of their strength, endurance and ability – and to really enjoy the freedom this brings.
- Saying 'No' should be done sparingly and mean something. It is short and clear, and works. Children also need to learn how to use it with authority and confidence.
- Exploring and labelling the children's feelings to empower them to communicate and set their own personal boundaries.
- Games that have set rules such as musical statues, musical chairs, attention builder (the look but not touch rule).
- Circle time games, pass an object. Speak when you are holding the object.
- Sand timers: pass resources to the next child when the timer runs out.

Fact Flash

Walls keep everybody out – boundaries teach people where the door is.

What can we champion at work?

Not everyone's boundaries will be known or familiar – some may seem quite irrational or even a bit silly and self-indulgent. They may also emerge suddenly and unexpectedly, and not conform to the majority view.

But they are relevant and deeply meaningful to the individual – this goes for both children and adults, and must be taken seriously. We often see the issues of boundaries emerge in conversations about risky play, or how we extend the children, or what some members of staff consider new and interesting while others consider them challenging and a bit uncomfortable, for example, how do you feel about a drag queen reading stories to children?

They could be related to any of the following: personal space, touch, volume of speech and laughter, politics, religion, intrusive questions, incompetence, time-keeping, over-sharing, weight issues, fertility issues, personal grooming, etc.

What behaviours can we champion? Can we be ... ?

Tolerant: Everyone's boundaries are particular to them and will be related to culture, life experience and upbringing. Tolerance is about not necessarily agreeing with someone's ideas or thoughts but accepting it, tolerating it and maybe even just going along with it to allow for overall harmonious relationships. Tolerance is about strength, seeing the bigger picture, seeing past differences and sometimes about doing what is right. It can be selfless; it can often be about putting other people's feelings and thoughts above our own. We also need to tolerate ourselves and find ways to accept ourselves and identify how we can improve or change. Ultimately, learning tolerance means we can learn about something we may have initially disliked. Being tolerant can build confidence and allow us to try something new.

Respectful: No one should be forced to share their reasons for having particular boundaries, unless it does not fit with the ethos of the organisation or may place children in an unsafe situation. A chat is useful at this point to avoid confusion or misunderstandings.

The issue of boundaries can also impact on your relationship with parents. They may take time to vocalise their concerns about some of the behavioural expectations related to their children and we know parenting styles can vary greatly.

Be patient on both counts.

Sensitive: Try to be sensitive with parents who may not agree with some of the behavioural expectations you have for their children and may not want them to experience risky play, go outdoors in the rain, get their clothes dirty, feed themselves, play and share with others or get dressed independently.

Understanding: This really comes with time, maturity and experience, and is something we should all aim for with each other, our children and our parents. It means being a bit flexible, adaptable and keeping at the very forefront of our minds what is best for that particular child on that particular day.

Simple activities to help children to begin to understand and manage boundaries

Here is a lovely activity with the children to help them begin to understand and manage boundaries.

The tower-building activity

- Take two groups of children and a number of items. The idea is to build the highest tower possible by using any item that they think would be suitable.
- Each child takes turns and selects any item they think would be suitable to create the largest tower.
- They then place these items on top of each other to create the tower.
- The observing children must sit patiently and not involve themselves with the selection and build until it is their turn.
- Tolerance is developed by allowing each child to select whichever item they want and the rest of the group having to tolerate their choice. Boundaries here are about waiting your turn and allowing one person to make their choice.

To ensure we feel strong, calm and in control of our decisions, try these following exercises. You can do them any time you need to focus.

You will need a cushion, a wall, or a tea towel.

1. Cushion: Hold a cushion across your chest. Take a deep breath in and as you blow out hug the cushion as hard as you can. When you need to breathe in again, take the pressure off and repeat.
2. Wall: Press-ups! Face a clean wall. Now place your hands at shoulder height on the wall as wide as is comfortable, breathe in and as you blow out lean as hard as you can into the wall. When you need to breathe in again, push your arms straight and repeat.
3. Tea towel: Roll up a tea towel into a snake shape. Stand with feet comfortably wide apart and hold onto each end of the towel. Pull it apart as hard as you can and begin to raise both arms until they are wide above your head. Keep your arms very straight and strong, breathe deeply in this position, look upwards then forwards.

Bitesize help

Read: Brené Brown (2017) 'Braving the Wilderness' published by Penguin Books, and Anne Katherine (2000) 'How to Set Boundaries Every Day' published by Simon Schuster.

Read: 'Boundaries' by Jennie Miller and Victoria Lambert.

Watch: www.ted.com/talks/shukla_bose_teaching_one_child_at_a_time

Listen: Ashley Whillans: 3 rules for better work-life balance | TED Talk

Check Out: www.ourmindfullife.com

Thoughts for today, and every day!

Be aware
Of what is
Unacceptable
Normalise saying 'No'
Do what's best for you
And know it is not your
Responsibility to sacrifice
Yourself for others

Start a journal

Journaling just means setting aside a little quiet, undistracted time to sit down and think about your life. It may include writing down a record of what happened that day, offloading about something that is really bothering you or noting something that has inspired you.

Chapter 5

Bounding with Energy

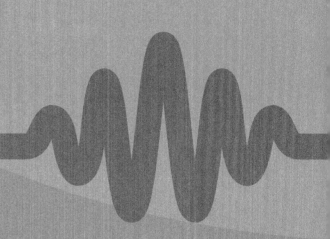

What do we know about energy?

Do you feel you ever have enough energy? Getting your energy balance right can be a challenge! How can we find enough to get through the day with some to spare?

Energy can be curiously elusive. It often seems to come and go without warning or explanation and, over a lifetime, energy level will fluctuate enormously – often the youngest and oldest in our society have it in abundance!

Energy is also something we envy and admire in others. We think people with lots of energy must be more productive, positive, successful, clever, accomplished and happier. But we all have a lot more energy than we imagine. Our reserve tanks ready for fight or flight as needed.

Energy levels are very personal; there will always be larks and owls – those who are wide awake at dawn or in the middle of the night. Useful to know when having a choice of shifts!

We also know about hares and tortoises – those who are life's natural sprinters or better suited to endurance activities: and 'radiators and drains' – people who give off lots of energy or absorb the energy of others. You will probably feel most comfortable with people who share your energy level and will often find those who aren't exasperating and exhausting.

Energy is also viewed differently by varying disciplines. In the therapeutic world, it is linked to the 'life force'. As Deepak Chopra writes: 'We live as ripples of energy in the vast ocean of energy.' Aligning energies and recognising the power of personal energy is seen as the key to self-discovery, growth and harmony.

Dr Tim Spector, in his book 'Spoon Fed', advises the following: 'As individuals, we need to tune in more to our own body's needs and these will change over time – life is one big experiment.'

Hormones can also have a huge impact on our energy levels. These are chemical substances that act like messenger molecules in the body. After being made in one part of the body, they travel to other parts of the body where they help control how cells and organs do their work. The hormones created and released by the glands in your body's endocrine system play a vital role in all phases of development, metabolism and reproduction.

This is a very useful exercise called 'STOP'. You can do it at any time to determine what your body needs – take as long as you feel works for you.

Sit on a chair with your feet placed hip-width apart and flat on the floor, close your eyes.

S Scan your body starting with your feet and working up to your head. Do you feel any discomfort/tightness or pain anywhere? Has anything emerged overnight or changed recently? Are you thirsty, hungry, tired, anxious, angry, distressed, excited, happy?

T Take a deep breath in through your nose and breathe out. Repeat till you feel calm and relaxed – maybe you have a favourite breathing exercise you could do at this point?

O observe – is there anything you need to concentrate on? Mobilising shoulders? Easing out your neck? Stretching your hands? Wiggling your hips? Yawning?

P Proceed with your day, be aware if you have discovered anything new and feel positive.

What do you notice about children's energy?

Children are generally very lively, but their energy levels can change quickly. They enjoy bursts of high energy for a few minutes followed by necessary short periods of rest and recovery. Their temperature control is not very reliable so they can easily get hot, tired and tearful. For maximum energy they need to be outside and active as much as possible and, like us, children also need time to be quiet, to recalibrate, renew, regroup and revive their energy. Certain fun activities will tap into our reserve tank, without our minds actually being very involved in the decision at all.

Children's energy levels are affected by much the same things as ours. For example, poor sleep routines and nutrition impacts on their ability to manage the day easily and happily. Extended exposure to stress and anxiety is also exhausting for children. They need to be physically active in the fresh air that will reliably boost their energy banks and sense of wellbeing.

Sometimes we can see the imbalance of energy levels between a parent and their child. The quiet, low-energy mum who honestly believes something is 'wrong' with her highly energetic child or the sporty, super-energetic dad who thinks there is a real 'problem' with his quiet, solitary, low-energy child. We can also find ourselves out of sync with children's

Fact Flash

Seventy per cent of our energy expenditure goes on just keeping us ticking over; this is the energy our cells need to burn to keep us alive. Ten per cent of this energy is used to digest food. Twenty-five per cent is used for physical activity, but ten per cent of this is used for small movements like sitting and standing. So we only have ten per cent to play with that must be used wisely. One third of our resting energy is allocated to brain function.

energy levels – and be suddenly cross and irritable – just be aware if and when this happens, it can often be linked to some of the issues mentioned previously.

What can we champion at work?

Working with young children can be demanding and exhausting, and we need to know what we can do to ensure we have enough energy to enjoy both our personal and professional lives. Teachers need to see each day as a brand-new day, as Maya Angelou puts it, 'It's a beautiful day. I have not seen one like this before.' Take each day as a brand new opportunity to ignite awe and wonder in children and their friendship groups – energy will follow passion every time!

In our settings, we often have to find a level of energy we don't actually feel, and this can be tough to manage. For some of us, our personal energy level aligns perfectly with what is needed professionally, but, for most, some conscious effort and application may be necessary.

If we are to support staff, we need to understand what impacts our energy levels negatively. For example, it could be something as simple as the environment being too hot or too cold, which can sap energy. This matters to both children and staff, so whether they are busy in the nursery or training all day, we must check that rooms are well ventilated, not too hot and stuffy.

Lack of fresh air can have a significant effect on energy levels, especially when you realise that oxygen levels inside are 11 per cent but they rise to 20 per cent when you are outside. So pop outside for a breath of fresh air and a boost of essential Vitamin D at the same time. Also, mixing with calm people, even for the briefest moment, will leave you feeling calm.

Energy fluctuates throughout the day and we all have a time when we may flag. After lunch or the 4.30pm dip, it affects everyone differently. Often this is when we go for the sugar hit and reach for the biscuits! But even though we get an instant energy boost, it really won't last for long and you may pay for it later with a sudden wave of tiredness and a waste of calories!

Staff working with children are usually very active, but for most of us screentime cannot be avoided. Too much sitting can be quite debilitating, places pressure on spinal discs causes shallow breathing and, if the room is stuffy, oxygen levels are depleted.

Try to move somehow every 15 minutes. Wiggle, yawn, stretch, tap your feet, shrug your shoulders and ease out your neck. Then every 30 minutes stand up, stretch up high and breathe deeply! If you are using a screen, remember they are very tiring for the eyes, so for every hour spent on screen, take a 10-minute break. Many employers also pay for an annual eye check, so check it out and book your test.

Instant energy boosters that work for you and your children

Take 'time out' somewhere in a calm and quiet space for five to 10 minutes and do one or more of the following activities – you will soon discover those that work best for you and the children.

- Rub yourself all over as vigorously as possible, start with your hands then shoulders, tops of thighs – you can do this standing or sitting.
- Pat yourself all over as hard as is comfortable.
- Clap your hands and stamp your feet – to music if you like.
- Run on tiptoes as fast as you can on the spot – pump your arms at the same time, breathe.
- March on the spot, get your knees as high as possible.
- Toe taps on a low step – as fast as you can.
- Sniff a cinnamon stick or peppermint essence – for some reason, this works!
- Get outside in the fresh air, even five minutes will be beneficial.
- Laugh.
- Being quiet and calm can also be energising, so try these two ideas:
  - learn to sing lullabies and sing them with the children they are very soothing;
  - lie on your back with your legs on a chair or up a wall, really sink into the floor then ease out your neck and breathe deeply and rhythmically.

Fact Flash

The three most-important factors in supporting energy levels are sleep, nutrition and movement.

SLEEP: Sleep is critical to our wellbeing, especially as we sleep on average for about one-third of our lives. We need between seven or eight hours, any more may just make you more tired and sluggish. We know that 30 per cent of the issues faced by GPs are directly or indirectly related to sleep difficulties. It's no surprise that 'TATT' (tired all the time) appears frequently in patient notes. Despite 30 per cent of patients taking some sort of medication for sleep problems, only 10 per cent admit to this during consultations, or even bring up the subject. In 2016, insomnia cost the UK Government £35.5 billion – a figure that will no doubt have risen due to the 2020 pandemic.

During sleep, the brain conducts a 'deep-cleaning' process using special glia cells to flush out metabolic debris using cerebrospinal fluid – this process maintains healthy brain function, washing plaque-forming proteins away that can, over time, lead to dementia.

Poor sleep makes the body produce more cortisol that affects sugar levels the following day. That affects the production of the appetite hormones – leptin and grelin – making people more likely to feel hungry and crave sweet food. Sleep-deprived people eat on average an extra 385 calories a day – one large slice of cake!

Growth hormones are released during sleep – and vital systems rest and recover, including the immune, nervous and endocrine systems. Muscles are also rested and rebuilt, infections are fought and memories consolidated. When sleep-deprived, only negative memories may be stored in the long-term memory area of the brain.

What can help us get a good night's sleep?

- Dim house lights from about 9pm.
- Try to go to bed before midnight and keep to a consistent time when you are naturally tired.
- Don't have TVs and computers on in your bedroom – the blue light they emit tricks the brain into thinking it is still daytime.
- Try not to use screens for 90 minutes before bedtime – the brain needs to start calming and winding down.
- Have a warm bath or shower.
- Make your bedroom as cool (18 degrees centigrade is optimal) and dark as possible.
- Make sure your bed is comfy and inviting. It is best to use natural and light fibres.
- Don't panic if you wake up at odd times in the night. Sleep goes in 90-minute cycles, so this is quite normal, and deep rest and sleep are both beneficial.

Nutrition for energy

Experts all agree that what we eat has a significant impact on energy levels. Did you know that 90 per cent of serotonin, the feel-good hormone, is created in the gut, so our mood can also be positively influenced. Eating well is important and we will look at nutrition throughout this book. Let's think about high-energy foods. Here are my top ten.

1. **Porridge** is one of the best sources of slow-releasing energy from low GI complex carbohydrates, to keep you going all morning. Also a great source of B vitamins, which are needed to convert food into energy.

2. **Spinach** is high in iron, magnesium and potassium. Iron transports oxygen around the body, needed for energy production. Magnesium plays a vital role in energy production, and together with potassium, is important for nerve and muscle function.

3. **Sweet potatoes** are a fantastic source of complex carbohydrates, along with iron, magnesium and vitamin C, needed for transporting fats into the cells of the body for energy production.

4. **Eggs** provide a complete protein containing all the essential amino acids, B vitamins, healthy fats and some vitamin D. They also provide choline, the precursor for the neurotransmitter acetylcholine, which activates skeletal muscle.

5. **Fruit has natural sugars**, which are quickly absorbed into the bloodstream for an instant pick me up (but without the 'sugar crash' you get after eating refined sugars). Invest in a fruit bowl – the more beautiful your fruit bowl the better stocked it will be – and the less likely you are to reach for unhealthy and energy-sapping sweet snacks.

6. **Green tea** contains some caffeine for an energy boost, but without the 'jittery' side effects of stronger caffeine drinks, such as coffee. Substitute herbal tea, such as peppermint, for more stimulating drinks such as coffee and tea and you may find your ability to be calm will be much enhanced.

7. **Nuts** are energy dense due to their high content of healthy fats.

8. **Soybeans** are high in protein, B vitamins, copper and phosphorous, which are involved in converting food into energy and releasing it into cells so it's available for use by the body.

9. **Fish** such as salmon, sardines and mackerel are an excellent source of complete protein, B vitamins, essential fats and vitamin D. A lack of vitamin D can cause low energy, muscle fatigue and low mood.

10. **Seeds** (squash and pumpkin seeds are an excellent source of protein, healthy fats and minerals involved in energy production – including manganese, magnesium, phosphorus and zinc. Be wary of products than claim to 'boost energy' – they never say how, when or why this may happen!

Fact Flash

Junk food

Try to avoid fast/junk food if possible; it is seductive and addictive, mainly because it is driven by the release of dopamine. This happens due to the sodium chloride in these foods, so salt is really the issue not sugar. We sweat over our entire bodies, so we need to replace salt that is not easily found in nature and was historically scarce – this explains why pizza not chicken and broccoli gives us such a buzz.

Protein supplements

These are used by 25 per cent of people in the UK – despite the fact most people exceed the daily recommended amount of protein. There is no difference between plant and animal proteins in building muscles, so no need to regularly eat steak and eggs! There also only needs to be 20 per cent protein in a chocolate bar for it to be sold as being 'high protein'. So yes, protein is a necessary source of energy, but be careful to get it from a natural and reliable source.

Energy Drinks

Be very careful with 'energy drinks' and 'sports drinks' – they are loaded with caffeine (one can of Red Bull contains as much caffeine as two expresso coffees). They often include high amounts of sugar and a range of chemicals that can become highly addictive.

Drinking water

300ml of water a day can increase our attention span by 25 per cent, boost our concentration levels and lower the prevalence of energy-sapping headaches and anxiety.

A quick quiz to help you get a handle on what supports or saps your energy.

Question	Answer What sort of actions work for you?	Question	Answer What sort of actions work for you?
What time of day do you feel most alert and energetic?		What do you do during this time?	
What time of day do you feel least energetic?		What do you do during this time?	
How much sleep do you get each night on average?		If you don't get enough sleep, how do you feel?	
Do particular people/places/things give you energy?		Do particular people/places/things take your energy?	

Bitesize help

Read: 'CALIBRATE' Christian Wilson – Amazon Publishing 2020

Read: 'If in doubt, wash your hair' – Anya Hindmarch Bloomsbury 2021

Watch: Films that give energy such as Chariots of Fire, The King's Speech, Cool Runnings, Despicable Me, Boy or Legally Blonde.

Listen: The Power of Human Energy: Angela Ahrendts www.youtube.com/watch?v=mZNIN31hS78

Check Out: Joe Wicks: The Body Coach TV or Do Yoga with Me

Thoughts for today, and every day!

Find opportunities to do fun things that give you energy – explore different possibilities inside the nursery and after work too!

Start a journal

Journaling just means setting aside a little quiet, undistracted time to sit down and think about your life. It may include writing down a record of what happened that day, offloading about something that is really bothering you or noting something that has inspired you.

Chapter 6

Friendships: The Chocolate Chips in Our Biscuits

What do we know?

Professor Jeffrey Hall from the University of Kansas suggests that the best single predictor for our psychological wellbeing and health, even for our risk of dying is the number and quality of friendships we have. He calls this the 'social biome' - the personal ecosystem of relationships and different daily interactions that shape our emotional, psychological and physical health. The most important factor in creating and maintaining a healthy 'social biome' is not the quantity of our daily interactions but their quality and variety. Being happily solitary is also a contributing factor and should always be included.

Professor Robin Dunbar – an expert in evolutionary psychology from Oxford University writes that:
'You're sitting at the centre of a series of expanding circles of friendship like ripples on a pond when a stone drops in. Just as each ripple is bigger and weaker than the previous one – each circle of friendship grows in size and decreases in the quality of relationship from your closest loved ones – to the weddings and funerals circle.' All interactions are embedded in an ever-extending, highly connected network of: family – community – nation – globe'

For most of us the ideal group of friends is about 150 people – but the usual range is between 100 – 250. Within our 'friends in general' group we will have an 'inner sympathy' group of around 15 people to whom we devote about 60% of our social effort.

The 'communication ladder' for our friendships goes like this:
- At the bottom: browsing social media with a minimal level of communication
- Next rung up: using direct messaging – sharing memes – Whatsapp/Facebook/Instagram etc
- Getting higher: phone calls and video chat/Facetime
- At the top: face-to-face conversations!

About how many from each rung do you have every day?

What type of communication gives you the most pleasure?

Professor Dunbar also suggests that five very close friends are the optimal number we need to minimise the risk of depression. These are the friends who will:
- Take your call at 4 am
- Offer you a place to stay at short notice
- Listen to you – go on – and on – and on ...
- Will drop anything to help you – whatever you need
- As the saying goes – they will 'overlook your broken fence and admire the flowers in your garden'

You may have some more examples to add from experience!

There is also a clear difference between the way introverts and extroverts manage their friendships.
- mIntroverts have fewer but stronger friendships – are very risk averse and really dislike losing friends for whatever reason
- Extroverts have a wider circle of friends but weaker relationships – they tend to

30%

the 20 plus age group – will change around 30% of their friends each year

rely on the volume of friends they have for support rather than a select few
- Overall – the 20 plus age group – will change around 30% of their friends each year as they relocate, get new jobs, settle down or become parents.

Our friendships were sorely tested during 2020 when suddenly we couldn't see people in person for months at a time and had to work out very quickly how friendships could be nurtured within an ever-changing situation; we got used to Zoom – Teams – facetime – even writing letters – and became very aware how much we all missed a lovely hug!

How did all this impact on our health and wellbeing?

The University College London 'Covid Social Study 2020' gained the following data from participating respondents:

- The number of people who reported feeling lonely remained stable – throughout the lockdowns – and when restrictions were lifted
- 22% said the quality of their friendships had deteriorated – this is likely to happen anyway within a few months if the previous level of contact is not maintained
- 50% thought their friendships had remained the same
- 15% thought their friendships had improved

So, what did the respondents think had changed?
- Their social circles had shrunk
- They felt their horizons had narrowed
- Many 'friendships of convenience' e.g. other school mums and wider work colleagues had been quietly shelved

Does small talk matter? Professor Hall advises that 'small talk' is actually very important. It is often dismissed as being irrelevant but just checking in with someone and sharing their space is 'critical to our sense of community and social nutrition.' Quick and friendly moments of daily 'incidental' contact can be very nourishing and have a much greater impact than you would imagine from the minimal energy expended.

Remember that the more comfortable you are with your friends talking about small things – the closer you will be for when the big stuff happens.

Our colleagues must trust that we will do the best job we possibly can whatever circumstances or challenges are presented. We must also trust our parents – that they will support us in our professional lives and back us up in the decisions we make.

Friendship and Trust
In his book 'The Thin Book of Trust' 2009 – Charles Feltman describes trust as 'choosing to risk making something you value vulnerable to another person's actions.'

In the Early Years world – the level of trust involved is truly exceptional – parents must trust us to care for and teach their children and ensure they are happy – well fed – well rested – that they enjoy their friends and activities – avoid accidents – and that we can provide appropriate intervention and support if/when needed.

Children must trust us implicitly – that we will be consistent – love them whatever – be kind and fair – sort things out – be their friend – confidant – playmate – source of interesting information and creator of adventurous play opportunities – chief negotiator with parents – and all round champion!

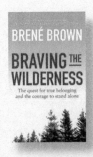

The American psychologist Brene Brown in 'Braving the Wilderness' suggests that the following seven elements are critical in any interactions where trust is a central requirement. Think of them in terms of your friendships – you may be surprised at some of your answers:

1. Boundaries: In terms of friendship, boundaries may be discussed and negotiated at any time. Setting and maintaining boundaries is important for our wellbeing (see chapter 4) so don't be too worried about being liked all the time - or disappointing others
Question: Do I respect my own boundaries and am I clear about them with my friends?

2. Reliability: This means doing what you say you are going to do and being aware of your own competencies and limitations. Try not to over-commit or over-promise just to please others or to prove yourself
Question: Am I a reliable friend – do I always do what I say I'm going to do?

3. Accountability: This includes being able to own your mistakes – to apologise if/when appropriate or necessary – to make amends – to 'let go of blame and stay out of shame'
Question: How good am I at owning my own actions within my friendships and being accountable for them?

4. 'Discretion'; This includes being able to keep confidences and knowing what can

be shared or not – never using gossip as a way to 'hotwire' friendships
Question: Do I always respect the confidences of my friends and do they treat my confidences with equal respect?

5. Integrity: This means staying true to your values – being courageous and choosing to do what is right
Question: Can I always stay true to my values even if they may make my friendships hard and uncomfortable sometimes?

6. Non-judgement: This means learning how to give and receive help – and knowing that you don't always have to be doing one or the other
Question: Can I ask for - or receive help from my friends without being judgemental about it?

7. Generosity: This includes trying to be as generous as you can towards the intentions and actions of your friends
Question: How generous am I towards my friends – do I always give them enough time – and do I properly listen to them?

Two fun activities that promote trust and friendship in a group

1. Pass the parcel – on the move ...

You can choose anything to be your 'parcel' – e.g. a teddy bear – bean bag – orange – coin – table-tennis ball – this is a great activity to encourage movement - and laughter!

- Define the space you are going to be moving in – you can stick masking tape on the floor – or use any available benches/chairs/tables
- The smaller the space - the more challenging this activity will be – so start off with enough space for everyone to feel comfortable
- Everyone must keep moving – walking forwards is simple – backwards more difficult – on tiptoes is easier than on heels
- Whatever apparatus you have chosen is passed from hand to hand between the group members – you can do this at waist height – or very high or low
- You can add music (like in the classic pass-the-parcel game) – then when the music stops – the person holding the apparatus chooses an action for the others to follow

2. Wool ball

This is a really good activity if you have a group that are new to each other – and are a little unsure of themselves.

Choose any topic you like to focus on – e.g. favourite food – song – book – holiday – celebrities: or 'things I am grateful for'

The group can sit comfortably in a circle or scattered – whatever suits best.

- Take a ball of wool – the first person holds the end tight and throws the ball to anyone they like – saying their name as they do so
- The person who catches the ball now contributes to the chosen topic
- When they have finished – they hold the string tight – and throw the ball to another person saying their name as they throw
- This continues until everyone has had a go – and the wool will be in a spider-web pattern
- Cut a piece of wool for each member of the group – they can tie this around their wrist or ankle – or just keep somewhere safe as a reminder of how it felt to be connected to everyone

What do we notice in children

Social relationships play an extraordinarily important role in children's development – they provide the context in which communication skills are acquired – language is rehearsed and refined – and they learn the habits, rituals and social nuances of cultural environments.

Of course, there are always challenges along the way: being with others for extended periods – fitting in and contributing to group activities – making and sustaining relationships – losing a friend – being excluded – failing to keep up or contribute to play – being rejected – all these can be demanding and tiring to manage for many children. We also need to help children nurture their friendships and support parents to understand their children's choice of friends.

They can also be very passionate about their likes and dislikes when it comes to friendships – and are often quite clear about their reasons. Being a good friend is a skill that must be acquired and practised and managing or amending expectations of friendship can sometimes be a painful and unhappy experience. So, they need to know that whatever happens, it will mostly be OK in the end, that they can trust us to do our best to facilitate and support their friendships,

that inclusion is a reality and matters profoundly and that being a good friend requires application, commitment and a certain amount of compromise.

For many children, the friendships they had already formed were sorely tested during the past year. Their usual modes of communicating through play – and doing things together to create and sustain relationships were not possible for extended periods of time. We know that the most physically competent and confident children have more mature social skills and a wider circle of friends – so may have recovered their social equilibrium more quickly - but children who are in the early stages of learning English – or whose language therapy was withdrawn may need extra support to regain their earlier level of language skills.

Fact Flash

Friendship and kindness thrive in a culture of courtesy. Don't assume your kindness and courtesy will automatically be reciprocated by everyone – but you will feel good about yourself if you can be a consistent and reliable friend whatever the circumstances.

What can we champion at work?

Friendship is critical to overall wellbeing – therefore supporting children manage their friendships and helping them to understand the expectations of relationships and avoid disappointments is very important. Many nurseries were closed during the pandemic and some parents were surprised that their children missed their friends so much. They also realised that their role in encouraging new friendships going forwards really mattered.

Our behaviour: Children are watchers and observers. They notice things and can immediately sense any tension or stress in the atmosphere, particularly in the way we behave and talk to each other. The tone of voice we use, our gestures, choice of words, how we respect personal space and create small acts of kindness and courtesy all communicate to children the skills needed for good interpersonal relationships.

Routines: that support kind behaviour help children to understand why this matters.

These are some ideas that promote kindness and friendship among children:

- Create a visual timetable around kind behaviour that includes some Makaton signs that staff can help children interpret if needed
- Golden rules to encourage acting kindly towards each other
- Establish a 'behaviour code' for routines that focus on eg: morning arrival, lunchtime, playing together and going home – this will help children understand the reasons for expected behaviours throughout the day
- Experiencing daily routines like helping friends to tidy up or providing comfort if appropriate will all help children connect with each other
- Mealtimes are a social time, with small table groups to encourage conversations.
- Role modelling how we take turns to listen

We also need to demonstrate and articulate to children and our colleagues how an inclusive culture may be built and nurtured.

This culture champions tolerance and understanding of individual differences ensuring no one is advantaged or disadvantaged for whatever reason.

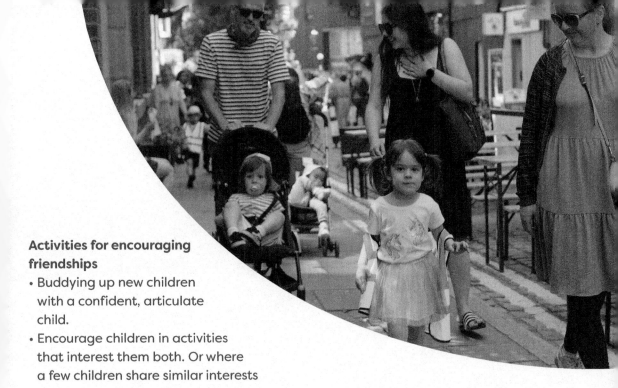

Activities for encouraging friendships

- Buddying up new children with a confident, articulate child.
- Encourage children in activities that interest them both. Or where a few children share similar interests

Read stories about friendships

- Teamwork activities that involve others such as-making playdough, constructing a model
- Group time discussions that emphasise taking turns to talk and listen
- Child led planning meetings that foster the sharing of ideas and properly listening to each other
- Teachers taking a step back sometimes to let a child make their own first steps towards being a friend

Creating a multi-generational approach. Some pedagogies such as the LEYF pedagogy has built in a multi-generational approach underpinned by:

- Extending the hand of friendship
- Building harmonious relationships
- Showing kindness to the many different communities and people living all around us.

If the nursery is to be a catalyst for community engagement - what can we do that shows children the value of friendship and neighbourliness in the community? Here are a few ideas.

- Visiting local elderly people and connecting with them over zoom when you can't visit.
- inviting children's' grandmothers in for tea
- Including families in local festivals and celebrations
- Organising regular visits - always saying hello when out on walks
- Bringing home made treats to the Big Issue seller

Thoughts for today, and every day!

'Share your smile with the world – it is a symbol of friendship and peace.'
'Friends are like stars – you don't always notice them – but you know they are there.'

Bitesize help

Read: 'Teacher wellbeing and self-care' – Adrian Bethune and Emma Kell – Sage publications – 2021

Watch: https://www.headspace.com/bbc

Listen: Podcast June podcast with Norma Raynes

Check out: www.jabadao.org/courses/the-feeling-of-me www.annafreud.org

Start a journal

Journaling just means setting aside a little quiet, undistracted time to sit down and think about your life. It may include writing down a record of what happened that day, offloading about something that is really bothering you or noting something that has inspired you.

Chapter 7

All About Our Backs

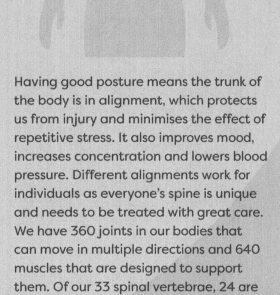

What do we know about backs?

Posture is not about being able to walk easily with a book on your head and keeping clean and tidy. It is active, dynamic and highly individual. Posture changes all the time in response to three elements: comfort (are we in pain anywhere), safety (are we in danger of any kind) and function (what we are doing physically). The purpose of posture is to help us best complete a physical task like standing, walking or running, and to keep our heads in the right position for optimum balance. It is primarily to do with how we perform and feel – not how we look.

Having good posture means the trunk of the body is in alignment, which protects us from injury and minimises the effect of repetitive stress. It also improves mood, increases concentration and lowers blood pressure. Different alignments work for individuals as everyone's spine is unique and needs to be treated with great care. We have 360 joints in our bodies that can move in multiple directions and 640 muscles that are designed to support them. Of our 33 spinal vertebrae, 24 are able to rotate, slide, extend and bend.

Back pain is one of the most common reasons for doctor visits, and lower back pain is now a leading cause of disability worldwide. Because the reasons for back pain are so many, varied and often difficult to determine, only 10 per cent of doctor visits result in a diagnosis. Most sufferers will recover in time if they rest, remain moderately active and keep moving gently, although a small percentage may develop a chronic long-term problem that results in constant pain and limited mobility.

Around 80 per cent of adults will experience back pain at some point in their lives and in the Early Years sector, it rises to 82 per cent. On average, adults take 14 days off work per year with back issues and those aged between 25–34 years old take the most. All this costs our economy around £26 billion per year!

In many ways, we are lucky working in Early Years because generally we are not sitting at a screen unable to move for hours on end. But we are lifting, leaning, shifting, carrying, pushing, pulling, reaching, twisting, rocking and getting up and down throughout each day. We need to be strong and pain-free to do our jobs properly, so we must have strategies and measures in place to ensure our lives are not disrupted by back pain that could be prevented.

What can we do every day to prevent back pain?
- Move as much as possible all day every day and make the most of joining in with nursery activities like the parachute game, which is brilliant for bending, stretching and laughing.
- Use available doorframes to stretch and realign your back. Every time you walk through one, reach up with both hands to touch the top.
- Drink enough water to hydrate the spinal discs, an extra cup per meal will really help.
- Move somehow every 30 minutes for 30 seconds. If having a static day, stretch, yawn, wiggle, walk on the spot, shake out hands, arms and legs.
- Take the stairs whenever possible, place hands on hips to make it harder.
- Practice turning slowly both ways for a count of eight to challenge your balance.
- Stand on one leg when you brush your teeth.
- Gently manipulate your neck and shoulders on waking – do this through the day and before bed.
- Check you are wearing comfortable footwear, it makes a big difference to how you stand and move.
- Check you are wearing the right-sized bra – this can also affect your posture and back health.
- Make sure you are not carrying a heavy bag on one shoulder every day. Try a rucksack or cross-body bag instead.
- If you wear varifocal glasses, check they are not creating extra neck tension.
- If you ever get the chance to swim, this is a wonderfully strengthening activity for the back.

What do we know about children's backs?

Young children are the perfect example of 'posture in action'. Much of their wriggling and fidgeting is necessary body recalibration and a means of getting comfortable, very rarely is it to do with being naughty or disruptive.

Unless they have had an accident or there is a significant medical issue, most children will not experience muscular-skeletal disorders (MSD) or back pain. If they enjoy a wide and varied diet of movement opportunities based on the foundation skills we have looked at previously, they should gain the overall strength, balance, co-ordination and agility to happily engage in whatever physical activities are open to them.

Children's posture can be affected by the following issues, so be aware of:
- Toothache/earache/headache – can seriously affect balance and posture and create tension in the neck and jaw.
- Constipation – they will sit clutching their tummy and curled over, tensing their neck and shoulders. They may also wriggle more when sitting.
- Eyesight – will affect balance and can provoke tension in the neck and shoulders, safety may be an issue.
- Overweight/obesity – carrying excess weight prevents children from safely joining in many physical activities and they may also experience pain in their hips, knees and feet.
- Shoe size – wearing the wrong-sized shoes (affecting 26 per cent of children) will affect balance and safety, particularly when moving at speed or climbing.
- Sitting – sitting cross-legged means they cannot naturally recalibrate their bodies or move into more comfortable positions.

What message will we champion at work?

Practising some of the very early movement skills with children is a fantastically effective way to support adult posture and maintain general musculoskeletal health. They provide the perfect way to maintain the overall body strength, balance, co-ordination and alignment that keeps us functioning and moving without fear of injury.

Fact Flash

More-confident people have better posture – and few pennies in your pocket will make you stand two inches taller!

Reviewing and revisiting these skills is useful for us and our children, and they are fundamental to ensuring we can operate pain-free, knowing our bodies will not 'let us down'.

Rolling is one of the very first 'big' movement skills to be acquired. It is a comforting and economical movement that gives the back a really good stretch. Babies love rolling, so get down on the floor with them and practise together whenever possible! Older children will also benefit as a lot of body strength is needed to keep arms and legs straight when rolling sideways.

Crawling is also a really good movement for our backs. Get onto your hands and knees with the children and gently do a few 'Cats and Cows' or follow the cat in our favourite stretch book, 'The Purrfect Pawse'! Arch up, then drop your back and wiggle your hips side to side. You can also rock your body forwards and backwards onto your heels, as you see babies doing when they are just beginning to think about crawling.

Balancing every day is essential to challenge the muscles that keep us upright. Having good balance determines how independent we can remain as we age and helps prevent injury and keep us safe. Lift and lower your heels while you help the children brush their teeth.

Stretching with the children whenever possible helps strengthen back muscles and mobilises the spine, so aim to join in properly if they are enjoying a yoga session, even if you are not leading it.

Some more ideas
- Do an active risk assessment in your setting that supports what you know about back health and good posture. Have some coloured stickers handy, now slowly look around each room and determine where you may have to be particularly careful about looking after your back. Identify tasks and activities that involve lifting, carrying, stacking. Put a sticker where it can be seen so everyone is aware and have an agreed plan if anyone knows they will need extra help at specific points.
- Provide a water fountain or a jug of water and a selection of herbal teas so staff can keep hydrated through the day.
- Create some fun and easy movement opportunities each day that everyone can join in: doing star jumps after breakfast or stretches before lunch could signal transitions; walk along a line of masking tape stuck on the floor; when entering or leaving, reach and touch stickers placed randomly on the wall whenever passing.

Thoughts for today, and every day!

Check the age of your bed mattress and if it is properly supporting your back. A change of mattress is recommended every seven years.

Bitesize help

Read: 'Playing with Movement' Todd Hargrave: Better Movement 2019

Watch: www.csiortho.com
https://www.youtube.com/watch?v=VDf43fOTH1E

Listen: https://apple.co/2YrigL2

Check Out: Charity Backcare website: https://backcare.org.uk/ http://www.nhs.uk/Livewell/workplacehealth/Pages/Backpainatwork.aspx

Start a journal

Journaling just means setting aside a little quiet, undistracted time to sit down and think about your life. It may include writing down a record of what happened that day, offloading about something that is really bothering you or noting something that has inspired you.

Chapter 8

Making Kindness Your Modus Operandi

What do we know?

The zeitgeist is often captured through objects such as mugs with slogans. 'Be Kind' is one such message which seems to capture a defining spirit of our history. The mugs suggest we want to be more sensitive to each other, show more empathy and behave in a kindly way.

The flip side of slogan messaging is that these become clichés and the messages meaningless, empty and posturing. So, you can feel good and look like you are doing the right thing just by making yourself a cup of tea, to "keep calm and carry on."

The clearest example of this appeared on social media when the hashtag #bekind was created in response to an event that caused a storm of anonymous, destructive and overwhelmingly negative publicity about someone who was no longer alive and therefore could not respond. Did any of those stickers, badges, mugs and t-shirts make any difference to people's behaviour? Did we become kinder?

It's no secret, being kind is good for your health. According to medical science, it can make us feel happier, improve our mood and lower our blood pressure. Being kind comes with a serotonin kick and neuroscientists can also detect the warm glow that comes from doing something rewarding and activates the striatum part of the brain. Better still is that seeing someone else smiling or being kind automatically activates the same areas of our own brain, as if we experienced the emotion for ourselves. It really is a case of smile and the world smiles with you.

Kindness and empathy go hand in hand but they are not the same thing.

Empathy is the ability to perceive, understand, experience and respond to the emotional state of another person. Empathy attunes us to the needs of individuals, so we are able to step into their shoes. Social empathy connects us to the realities and injustices experienced by other groups and involves both challenging our perspectives and recognising the limitations of our own viewpoints. Social empathy leads us to shared understanding of our reciprocal responsibilities to one another.

Kindness means extending a generous 'benefit of the doubt' towards someone with whom you have already empathised. It demands that you do something, not just say it. Kindness comes in many and varied forms; verbal, physical, silent, demonstrative. They are all relevant and they all matter. Being kind moves you from saying you feel sorry for a homeless person to giving them food.

The very first person you should be kind to is yourself. This can sound selfish but actually this is essential to secure and maintain your emotional and physical wellbeing. When we feel soothed and content and peaceful we feel safe, we are confident enough to look outwards beyond the immediate needs of survival and are able to live in a more connected and harmonious way with those around us. In other words, if you can be kind to yourself, then you can be kind to others.

Fact Flash

Engaging in acts of kindness produces endorphins, the brain's natural painkiller! Consistently kind people have 23% less cortisol (the stress hormone) and age two times slower than the average population!

Kindness means looking after your overall health and wellbeing, eating well, enjoying being physically active and having a hot bath or shower, sleeping properly, looking forward to simple things like a TV or radio programme, a phone call, a good book, a manicure, a visit or finding a new plant to pot. Remember – we are not 'the survival of the fittest' – but 'the survival of the nurtured.'

If you know how good this makes you feel, then you will know how to be kind to others. Simply treating yourself with a little more kindness and compassion can also yield significant benefits, including suffering far less mental and physical pain. Reward yourself. You have the best job in the world and those children love you!

Activity Time

Take this simple feelings quiz. It's a useful activity because often common threads emerge that you can think about and explore further.

I feel – these are 'positives'

HAPPY when I ...

GENEROUS when I ...

LOVED when I ...

VALUED when I ...

EXCITED when I ...

ENERGISED when I ...

NURTURED when I ...

SUPPORTED when I ...

I feel – these are the 'negatives'

ANGRY when I ...

POWERLESS when I ...

SAD when I ...

RESENTFUL when I ...

ANXIOUS when I ...

UNDERMINED when I ...

DEFEATED when I ...

EXHAUSTED when I ...

- What do you notice about your positives? –Do they include people/physical activity/hobbies/nature/food/being alone?
- What do you notice about your 'negatives? Do the same situations/people/experiences appear more than once?
- Being kind to yourself involves doing and experiencing things that make you feel good about yourself – think about WELLNESS (you) and your–PURPOSE (what you like to do) and your COMMUNITY (who do you like to hang out with and where do you fit in best).
- Many cultures include particular kindness rituals around major life events e.g. birthdays and weddings – do these feature in any of your answers here?

Fact Flash

Committing acts of kindness lowers blood pressure. Acts of kindness create emotional warmth, which releases a hormone known as oxytocin. Oxytocin causes the release of a chemical called nitric oxide, which dilates the blood vessels. This reduces blood pressure and, therefore, oxytocin is known as a "cardioprotective" hormone. It protects the heart by lowering blood pressure.

What do you notice about children being kind?

Our role in encouraging kindness starts when the children arrive and we sing the welcome song, the "How are you today" song or lead a circle time. It gives voice to feelings, but it also encourages empathy which converts to kindness when children look out for a new child or a sad child. Children can be very kind. They will help each other and understand when another child needs more time or support. They will find tissues for a crying child, respond to a child with additional needs, recognise the support a younger child might need to complete a task. As adults we are often very touched by how children's empathy translates into active kindness.

Early Years is a place where we work hard to support children learn to share and cooperate. We set the scene for collaboration and negotiation within the parameters of children's ages and staff understanding of their stage of development. We create a calm, soothing environment with a range of activities and resources that help promote kindness.

Of course, this begins with how we look after our environment, whether watering plants or feeding our stick insects. We also help children to express their feelings. How we teach two-year-olds with limited language about kind words is different to developing rules with children aged 4 and 5. Try reading Vivien Gussin Paley's You

Can't Say You Can't Play as an example. Children can also be very unkind to each other, and they generally know when they are being like this and have upset someone. They know that telling tales, not sharing, pushing, shouting "you are not my friend" and disrespecting their environment are all examples of being unkind. Staff must try to understand the circumstances and help them negotiate, apologise, and self-regulate so they can manage their emotions and learn from the experience.

Tiredness, discomfort and emotional maturity all impact on how children behave. Two-year-olds are much less tolerant than children aged 4 and its our job to help them respond well, to acknowledge their moments of failure and praise their efforts to manage the circumstances where they were unkind.

Some years ago, we noticed the children were being unkind to each other, We had a serious planning meeting with them and expressed our dismay. We talked about why kindness mattered and how it helped their brains smile.

The children engaged and began to think about what this meant for them. As an adult team we did not respond with a usual set of "golden" rules but re-framed the routine and the daily vocabulary around kindness. We actively used words such as modest, helpful, generous, courteous and considerate on a daily basis and noted examples of being kind, praising the children for showing spontaneous kindness such as helping a smaller child, running to get help, picking a toy up for a baby and all the little actions that once observed gave everyone a warm feeling.

Create a Tree of Hearts and give hearts to children that you see demonstrating kindness. Suggest that children give hearts to others too. Get involved in 'Random Acts of Kindness' Day or other similar events. Make a 'kindness book' with the children and place it in the book corner for everyone to share.

Having a multigenerational element to your pedagogy supports you to connect with local communities of all ages and backgrounds as part of the day. Nurturing those relationships builds kindness and in doing so strengthens the children's words to describe kindness and builds their understanding of the concept of kindness.

Remember kindness and empathy can be taught and learnt. There are many examples of this from making friends with the local Big Issue sellers and bringing

them treats to organising donations to the local Food Bank and raising money by decorating tea towels, making calendars, propagating plants in empty tins to sell for a chosen charity. Walk about and smile and say hello to people who might be lonely. Organise a litter pick locally. Visit the local elderly people's home for a sing song. One nursery has created a partnership between London and Ireland to celebrate their shared Irish heritage and use Zoom to keep in contact.

The list is endless, it just requires us to look around and see outside of ourselves. Once you start this, the children won't need much prodding as kindness is a natural human response.

A similar approach to the environment is supported through Green LEYF, an approach to sustainability designed to help children learn about their responsibilities to look after the world around them. Similar models include Planet Mark or OMEP Global Citizen programme.

What can we champion at work?

We are in the privileged position of being able to develop children's empathy and their ability to act with kindness towards themselves, their environment, and other people. It is a continual work in progress and something that over time we hope becomes an automatic response for them – it is simply how they are.

Teaching children about kindness, what it looks like and when and how to use it is good for children, staff and families and hopefully everyone they meet. Therefore, we need to create a 'culture of kindness' which means looking after staff wellbeing too. Kindness is catching – if we treat ourselves with kindness – this will be reflected in how we treat our environment (immediate and globally) – and how we interact with other people. Observing the positive impact of giving on the lives of others can elicit contagious feelings of joy.

At the heart of staff wellbeing is a sense of professional integrity and trust – feeling good about doing a good job. Children will notice every instance of kindness and empathy we demonstrate amongst our fellow teachers and with them. In order for our teams to be productive and for individual staff to feel safe and secure in the arms of the organisation we need to lead with kindness, empathy and fairness.

A foundation stone of teaching children about sociability and social functioning happens through making and nurturing relations. A multigenerational approach as part of the pedagogy means making every effort to connect with people of all generations. Through partnerships not only will we build harmonious relationships but also we can help reduce loneliness and isolation.

This is also known as "People, Communities and The World". This includes staff modelling kindness more explicitly with each other and using key words for the children to hear. Forming partnerships with Age Exchange or a homeless charity, being partners with Teens and Toddlers and visiting and supporting the local Food Bank all demonstrate practical ways of building kindness into the day which is good for children and staff.

Introduce children to the idea of random acts of kindness to encourage them to show kindness to their friends and families in unexpected ways. Make thank you cards, take out smoothies for parents during their morning rush, create magnets with their favourite kind words. Involve the chef. Have little kindness cards for the delivery drivers and the librarian. Another long list!.

Kindness is an essential ingredient that connects communities and children are wonderful catalysts.

Many young children live in very diverse and fast changing communities and we must help them find their place there.

The most important thing to remember when it comes to teaching kindness is to model the behaviour you hope to see in the children— be kind yourself and each other and they will be encouraged to mirror that kindness.

When you feel the need to be kind to yourself – try this '5 minute - 5 -4-3-2-1 senses meditation'
- Sit or stand – on a chair or against a wall – you need to feel supported
- 5 Look around and note 5 things you can SEE
- 4 Close your eyes and note 4 things you can FEEL
- 3 Keep eyes closed and note 3 things you can HEAR
- 2 Now note 2 things you can SMELL
- 1 Finally note 1 thing you can TASTE

Thoughts for today, and every day!

Kind thoughts - kind words - kind hearts

Bitesize help

Read: Developing Empathy in the Early Years by Helen Garnett (Jessica Kingsley Publishers 2018)

Read: Foundations of Being by Julia Manning-Morton Early Education 2017

Watch: https://www.headspace.com/bbc

Listen: EMPATHY - BEST SPEECH OF ALL TIME By Simon Sinek | Inspiratory - YouTube or https://www.ted.com/talks/emily_esfahani_smith_there_s_more_to_life_than_being_happy?referrer=playlist-how_to_notice_and_build_joy_into_your_life

Check Out: https://www.helpguide.org/articles/relationships-communication/making-good-friends.htm

Start a journal

Journaling just means setting aside a little quiet, undistracted time to sit down and think about your life. It may include writing down a record of what happened that day, offloading about something that is really bothering you or noting something that has inspired you.

Chapter 9

The Stress Factor

What do we know about stress?

We know, because we experience and feel it, that there is a big difference between the sort of stress that provides quite enjoyable pressure and stress that is continual, unmanageable and bad for us. 'Good stress' is the little bit of stress or pressure we often impose on ourselves that stretches us and provides the impetus to achieve, create and perform.

It is essentially composed of short-lived, controllable and often fun challenges – like going on a rollercoaster ride, speaking in public, sprinting for the bus or rock climbing. We generally manage these situations quite well because there is a defined beginning and end. 'Good stress' is really an essential part of normal development and a key element in mastering new skills and acquiring resilience.

But ...
Stress can also be toxic. This is where 'the demands on a person in any given situation exceed that person's resources or ability to cope'. Again, this will vary greatly between individuals, but the fundamental problem is that the ancient systems in the body that are designed to manage our reaction to stress (our fight or flight responses) behave in exactly the same way whether we are being chased by a bear, struggling to get the computer to work before a virtual meeting, or sitting in a traffic jam.

A system that was primarily designed for physical challenges now has to deal with continual emotional issues, a very different type of threat that results in the physical response to stress being completely disproportionate to the issues faced.

Without the option of running away very fast, which would effectively flush the stress hormones cortisol and noradrenaline from the body, these hormones linger as a toxic presence in our systems and can be very harmful.

When people say, 'I am so stressed, I have come out in hives', they are right! Stress can remain in the body and lie dormant until any of the following physical symptoms may appear: rashes, muscular fatigue, insomnia, eczema, raised blood pressure, migraines, palpitations and poor eating habits – it's your body's way of saying, 'enough'!

- Cortisol is really bad for our wrinkles because it prevents the skin from producing collagen and repairing itself.
- It also suppresses our immune system meaning we are more likely to pick up infections and viruses.
- Our hair can also be affected as noradrenaline knocks out the cells in our hair follicles that create pigment, so after a few days inactivation they go grey!

We need to find ways to manage stress that work well for us. Although we can't change our basic systems, we can definitely make changes to the ways we deal with stress by doing things that are positive and good for us. Give ourselves a break. Drink enough water to keep hydrated. Eat well, meaning lots of fruit, nuts, brightly coloured vegetables, not too much meat and dairy. Vitamin B12 is very important.

Move as much as you can throughout the day, keep joints mobilised and breathing even, note where you may hold tension in the body (check hands, neck, shoulders and jaw) and do something about it ASAP, not hours later.

Sleep, rest and leisure are all vitally important. Researchers have found that puzzles, Lego, painting, box sets, walking, cleaning, swimming, making lists, playing music, knitting, dancing, yoga and laughing are useful coping mechanisms.

Spend time with any animal that you can handle, pat or stroke. The interaction between people and pets lowers cortisol levels and increases production of the feel-good hormone oxytocin. Big or small, feathered, hairy or smooth, just feeling attuned to an animal, breathing together and stroking and patting them rhythmically, is very calming and beneficial.

Dogs are particularly great as they also push you to exercise! Enjoy the daily walk, taking in nature and fresh air and meeting members of the dog community who will often stop to talk. So, dog walking provides an opportunity for social interaction too.

Keeping a 'stress diary' can be very useful. Knowing the main triggers of stress in your life, when and where you experience the most stress, who and what is involved and which strategies you use to cope; all these may change and evolve over time, but having a record to turn to may really help.

Fact Flash

We are 12 per cent more productive when in a positive mood.

The 2018 EYA report, 'Minds Matter', suggests that stress was caused by the demands of working in the Early Years sector, low status and often low pay, while having to multi-task at work while keeping the plates spinning at home too. The findings showed how much we were concerned:

- 25 per cent of Early Years staff are considering leaving the sector due to stress
- 44 per cent are stressed about work 'very often'
- 74 per cent are regularly stressed because of their jobs
- 23 per cent have taken time off work due to stress
- In the UK, overall, 602,000 cases of work-related stress were reported in 2018/9

74%
of people are regularly stressed because of their jobs

23%
of people have taken time off work due to stress

What do we notice about stress in children?

Babies in utero can be exposed to high levels of cortisol through the placenta. If a mother is stressed over a long period of time, raised levels of cortisol can put a serious strain on their baby's developing systems.

At around two years of age, intense connections are formed between the brain and the immune system, so if the brain is under severe stress at this time, the whole body will respond. Bodies do not forget significant stress and children's long-term physical health may be seriously impacted by early stressful experiences.

Raised cortisol levels have been found in very young children attending nurseries and remain high for up to five hours after returning home.

Children deal with stress in different ways – some are 'orchids' who are highly sensitive to environmental factors and suffer most in challenging conditions – others may be 'dandelions', who can flourish anywhere, are hardier and may be less sensitive to adverse circumstances.

Children coping with trauma and neglect can become hypervigilant or highly alert to any perceived threat. This can be seen in their behaviour, which may include difficulties in regulating their emotions and dealing with stressful situations, by withdrawing or being highly anxious.

The brains of children growing up in abusive or neglectful environments will definitely be shaped by adverse experiences. These brain changes may not lead immediately to obvious mental health issues and may effectively support children to survive their challenging circumstances. But real problems arise when the coping strategies they have formed for themselves that work in one environment, e.g. home, emerge as inappropriate and unusable in another, e.g. school.

We all know about the 'fight or flight' response to stress that we often see, but equally important is the 'disappear' option, when children 'dissociate', escape into an inner world, are super-compliant and people-pleasing and avoid conflict at all costs – these are the children whose stress triggers may be unknown or overlooked and therefore need careful observation.

Coping mechanisms may also be intensely physical. Children may express their anxiety and stress through regression and/or aggression, lip sucking, bed-wetting, shouting, biting and performing repetitive behaviours like rocking, walking on tiptoes or squeezing their eyes tight shut.

Remember that short-term elevated stress levels immediately decrease activity in the areas of the brain that deal with response-planning and inhibition – so attention and learning will be negatively affected.

What can we champion at work?

A bit of pressure is fine because it can provide a challenge, keep us 'on our toes' and make us more efficient. But long-term wear and tear on the system, known as the 'allostatic load', must be managed and lessened whenever and wherever possible. Of course, this may change from day to day, but working out what makes the difference for us as individuals between 'coping' and 'struggling' is critical.

Be aware of 'burnout'. Think of it like sunburn, by the time you've been harmed, it's too late! Enjoying the heat of the sun can be positive, but knowing what makes up your Factor 50 protection screen is essential. This will include many of the suggestions made in previous chapters that you may have journaled already. Start from your feet and end at the top of your head. What do you do to protect yourself from stress at each point as you move up your body?

Look out for your colleagues and if you note any of the following, be sensitive and understanding: excessive worrying over small things, experiencing unusual aches and pains, using negative language, not joining in for minor reasons, being very tired all the time, overall loss of confidence, sudden change in appearance or an overall decline in the quality of work.

Create cosy dens for the children in little corners. Use a large piece of material such as a bedsheet in a calm and neutral colour. Add cushions, baskets of jar lids with pictures of children's families stuck on them, soft toys, a basket filled with homemade books about each child and their families, scented bags and some battery-powered twinkly lights. Children can get overwhelmed with the busyness and noise of the day and may need to take a few minutes out to recalibrate and reset.

For children who are struggling to connect with other children, they may enjoy using hula hoops with ribbons attached to visually create their own space. This can also work by providing cardboard boxes that they can sit in with their favourite toys. Then the teacher can slowly introduce other children to play alongside the child, who may need more time to adjust to the busy nursery routine.

The role of the teacher is to facilitate and create the environment that best supports children's different needs. These will include feeling safe, in control, recharging when necessary and building up enough courage and confidence to fully integrate with their peers. They must also learn the norms and expectations of play and the rules of the setting.

Joining in with the children's art activities can be a great stress releaser. Wallow in the feel of gloop or clay or playdough as you stretch and knead and stir and mix and appreciate the sheer pleasure that this gives to children. Enjoy it with them and absorb yourself in the experience. Explore a new idea like Hikaru Dorodango, a Japanese art form in which earth and water are moulded, then carefully polished to create a delicate shiny sphere, resembling a billiard ball.

Sit with the children on the sofa and practice massaging your eyebrows by putting pressure on the relaxing acupuncture points around the forehead then moving your fingers in an outward motion to the end of the brow. You can also teach them how to gently massage their ear lobes and lightly pinch around the outer part of the ear. They will all enjoy doing this and you can introduce lots of new words at the same time.

Move! Being physically active plays a consistent and significant role in reducing stress. Move even if it feels like the last thing you want to do, as the endorphins generated will make you feel so much better and help you sleep well at night. You can join in all the children's activities in ways that suit you, so when they have a yoga session or are running outside, just give it a go! Children love it when you move with them and it's always good to laugh!

Activity
Spotting the spots: This is a really good anti-stress activity for you and the children that you can do at home or in the nursery.
1. Have some green, blue and orange dot stickers handy. Choose the best places to put them, you can change them around whenever you like, they are just there as useful reminders.
2. Every time you see a:
Blue sticker – this means time to move, stretch, wiggle, check any tense areas of the body, bounce and energise

Green sticker – this means taking a few minutes to breathe deeply, focus, feel calm, settled and 'mindful'

Orange sticker – this means time to focus and be positive – say to yourself: 'Today may I be ... ', 'I am feeling ... ', 'I achieved this today ... '

Further ideas to manage stress

Learn about how the child's brain and its interdependent systems work together to navigate a complex physical and social world.

How adults respond to children is crucial. Learn to step back and reflect, so you help reduce a stressful situation not add to it. Understand the 'power of the pause' and breathe.

Make sure you have resources that help both the children and staff identify and respond to stress. There is a range of books available, such as the set of six children's emotional education picture books written by Kay Brophy. The six books have been designed to help children understand and communicate their emotions through fun characters in the stories that include: The Sad Skeleton, The Frightened Fairy, The Happy Hobgoblin, The Angry Alien, The Disgusted Dragon and The Surprised Sprite. At the end of each book is a 'Did you know?' section for the adult that suggests ways in which they can best support children's social and emotional development.

Teach the staff about the amygdala hijack and different ways of responding to stress triggers, e.g. when you need to have a difficult conversation, figure out your own support strategies, is it a quick walk, a cup of tea or perhaps some role play with a supportive colleague?

It's marvellous how quickly many worries dissolve if you take time to write them down in full. When you later review what you've written, quite often things seem less painful and easier to manage. Time can give you a different perspective and the journaling option included in each chapter may offer a good opportunity to try this approach.

Try to carry out tasks as they arise and in order of priority. Remember the wisdom of Benjamin Franklin who warned us not to put off until tomorrow what you can do today. Letting tasks build up adds stress and then we become overwhelmed and don't know where to begin. Instead, the list goes round and round in your head and leaves little space for calm.

Avoid exposure to doom and gloom news stories as they are inclined to cause you to panic. Watch enough to keep you informed, but balance your viewing with feel-good programmes.

Talk to people you like and trust in any way that works for you. Most people prefer face to face, but video calls can be a useful alternative. Some organisations purchase an employee assistance package for staff.

Find a safe or appropriate space where you can be alone and practice a few breathing techniques or stretch and be calm.

Think about small touches that show you care. Have a good range of teas, coffee and a bowl of fruit accessible to everyone and provide a cake or a chocolate treat – sometimes, a little of what you fancy does you good!

Have a 'pamper box' in the bathroom. It is often the only place you can go to de-stress so make it a pleasant experience. Don't stick too many scary notices on the back of each bathroom door!

Staff really appreciate a handwritten card or little treats to say thank you. Honestly, we don't say thank you enough in the Early Years! We think we have to solve world peace before we deserve a compliment and then we struggle to accept it and just graciously say 'Thank you' back – why?!

Having team get-together days with colleagues is always a good plan. Go bowling, have a fish supper, go for a walk, go charity shop hunting – whatever suits your team. It's often a good opportunity to clear the air and enjoy time together as adults away from the demands of work.

Thoughts for today, and every day!

Children need to be SAFE –
SEEN – SECURE and
SOOTHED. And so do we.

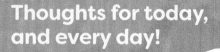

Bitesize help

Read: 'What happened to
you? Conversations on Trauma,
Resilience and Healing' by Bruce
Perry and Oprah Winfrey – Flatiron
Books 2021

Watch: www.limeade.com/
resources/blog/3-ted-talks-to-
help-you-de-stress/

Check Out:
www.uktraumacouncil.org

Super Apps: BBC Headspace /
Calm / Aura / Insight Timer /
Ten Percent Happier

Take the Happiness Pulse https://
bit.ly/3kjfhvR

Visit: www.global-journey.com –
for wonderful calming music

Start a journal

Journaling just means setting aside a little quiet, undistracted time to sit
down and think about your life. It may include writing down a record of what
happened that day, offloading about something that is really bothering you or
noting something that has inspired you.

Chapter 10

Resilience

What do we know about resilience?

A dictionary definition of resilience is: 'The ability to be happy and successful again after something bad has happened.'

But resilience appears in many shapes and forms. People are considered 'resilient' if they can cope with difficult events or circumstances, objects are described as 'resilient' if they can withstand compression and recover their original shape, countries are deemed 'resilient' if their infrastructure works in the face of climate change or economic collapse and companies claim to be 'resilient' if their financial systems can withstand trading highs and lows.

"There is no happiness except in the realisation that we have accomplished something"
Henry Ford

Seven elements of resilience

Historically, resilience is present in the Hindu concept of 'karma' and 'redemption' in Christianity. Music and literature are also full of heroes and heroines overcoming great trials and suffering to achieve something memorable and meaningful for themselves and others.

On an individual level resilience has been defined as:
- Steering through adversity and learning from it
- Being able to function relatively normally in adversity
- The capacity to prepare for, recover from and adapt in the face of stress, adversity, trauma and tragedy
- The ability to recover from setbacks, adapt well to change and keep going in the face of adversity
- Building resilience is about identifying the strategies that help you cope better

All these definitions include adversity, but this is relative, and it means very different things to different people. What constitutes adversity for one person may feel like a minor issue to another. Essentially, events themselves do not cause trauma but how we react to them is the central issue.. Resilience has much to do with inner strength; it can be well supported by physical strength and the combination of the two can make for a very powerful and personal 'brick wall.'

"Positivity is like a boomerang. The more we put out there, the more it comes back to us."
Jon Gordon

What does resilience involve?

Resilience is not something you either have – or don't have – think of it more like a muscle that needs to be tested little and often to gain the strength and flexibility needed to work at an optimum level.

Resilience is acquired over a lifetime of experience and starts from day one – it is an essential life skill. It involves a lot of mental and behavioural agility that helps us adapt and react appropriately to different events or circumstances and the ability to choose the best skills for each situation. Being resilient requires a level of self-efficacy which means believing that we can create and navigate our own path through adversity.

It can be expressed in many different ways that include visible skills, attributes and activities but may emerge through profound silence and contemplation. It also covers accessing the physical, social, psychological and cultural resources that may help. These resources can be historical and faith-based and used individually or collectively.

Being realistic means keeping a proper sense of perspective about the cause of adversity. The situation will not be permanent; it is not all about you; it will not affect absolutely everything in your life; will it really matter in five years time?

Resilience is all about being realistic – and flexible.

Being flexible means knowing what you can do to help yourself that is active and positive; anticipate and prepare for possible adversity – some events emerge from nowhere but others may be looming for a while before they actually appear.

In your own life – you will encounter many and varied ways of dealing with adversity - people need to do what works best for them culturally, physically and emotionally.

Can you think of people you know who have coped very differently – what did they do – and did it work for them?

We know that these three areas cause particular stress and require resilience to manage: relationships, parenting and money. Many organisations help their staff to deal with money issues by connecting them to **www.fairfinance.org** or having an employee assistance programme that points them in the right There are also national helplines such as **www.nationaldebtline.org** and **www.stepchange.org.uk**

How do we react to failure?

Failing is part of real life. Everyday can bring failures some small, some spectacular. Relationships fail, contracts fail, activities fail, projects fail, and recipes fail – we can fail exams and driving tests – but also fail to send a birthday card, call a friend, say hello or give a much-needed hug.

Without experiencing failure we won't get to grow and learn, often in very unexpected ways. Success is never guaranteed or the only outcome – it is simply part of the learning landscape that reminds us our efforts were worth it.. Failure is equally important because it can help us recalibrate the way we think about things and plan our next move.

When dealing with failure do you recognise any of these reactions? This is a good topic for group discussions! Also notice if any of your children behave in similar ways.

Accepting that mistakes are an essential part of learning requires patience from us , trust from our children and often a great deal of humour from everyone!

- Blame yourself: Do you immediately say " it is all my fault – it's a disaster – I'm a failure"
- Blame others : Do you immediately shout - " its not my fault . Nothing to do with me gov!"
- Catastrophise: Do you immediately cry - "oh no everything is a disaster" !
- Feel helpless: Do you immediately weep - "oh there is nothing I can do to change anything"
- Run away: Do you immediately announce - "I'm out of here"
- Deny: Do you immediately refuse to talk about it - "that never happened"

Activity Time

Activity: Name – Tame – Reframe ...

This is a really useful exercise to do if you need a framework to think things through – it can be applied to many different scenarios.

1. Name the problem:

What is the issue? – it's a disaster – I'm a failure – general wallowing – write it down or say it however it appears to you at the time

2. Tame the problem:

Why am I thinking like this? – is this something I always do – how can I make the issue less overwhelming and create 'bite-size' manageable pieces

3. Reframe the problem:

What are the positives I can gain from this? – what can I learn – are these lessons useful in any way

Eating The Elephant : Bite by Bite

First Bite : When adversity strikes - Commit to small and manageable goals each day. Keep to a trusted daily routine and build three positive things into your day that make you feel stronger and more in control. For example, take 10 minutes to read a book or listen to the radio, do a breathing exercise, have a shower or wash your hair! Try to be kind to yourself and keep clean, rested, fed and watered. You are your own house plant.

Think:

This day will be/ has been OK

I can/will cope

I will/did manage

Fact Flash

Everyone has an inherent ability to cope with difficult and challenging events, and 2 out of 3 people actually do so. We just have to watch out for the other third.

What do we notice in children?

Resilience comes from a mix of nature, nurture and culture. From birth onwards, children need close, consistent and loving relationships with their primary caregivers. As they grow and develop a minimum of five people will be needed to create the 'quilt of relational experiences' that keeps them safe, secure and soothed long-term. They learn very early about dependency and trust, who to trust who not to trust, and who they can rely on.

In children, coping with disappointment starts early. Babies want to be fed or picked up but may have to wait a bit. They need to roll over, crawl, stand and walk but this all takes time to achieve and their efforts are not always immediately successful.

Every time children make mistakes new synapses grow in their brains. They need to experience and manage a range of emotions every day in a caring and supportive environment. Learning to make mistakes without thinking it's the end of the world is a really important skill and one that can be usefully transferred from the physical domain.

Gaining physical skills requires determination, focus, perseverance and courage – children need to be adaptable and patient as their strength and balance begins to support more complex and mature skills. Being physically active is a brilliant way for children to acquire resilience – because it happens entirely on their terms and can be personal or collaborative in nature.

As they learn to swim, cycle or play with a ball resilience will be needed to ensure they continue to practise and refine these skills despite the many inevitable setbacks. Through participating in different games and sports they will learn to win and lose graciously , accept disputed results and understand that life may just be very unfair some days!

Fact Flash

One of the best ways we can develop resilience is to do things that make us happy. Write down 5 things that make you happy and do them!

What message will I champion at work?

How we support children is not that different to how we support staff. Both need to build confidence to respond to challenges in a positive way. Create a culture of warmth and kindness where they can learn together. Build trust with children. It is an immensely protective factor and critical to keeping those resilience muscles nicely flexed!

Having the right coping tools is essential – so help staff and children gain:

- Knowledge, skills and experience –all acquired over a lifetime and unique to everyone – be careful of 'deep-diving' online – it doesn't always help
- Confidence – that you can and will get through this – in one piece – and mainly OK
- Adaptability – you know that what you are doing is the best way for you at this particular time
- Support – this may change over time and in response to different events – but have a portfolio of different possibilities that work for you – both real and virtual
- Environment – this will include family, work, community – virtual communities and online support sites

The best thing parents and teachers can do is to teach children to love challenges, be intrigued by mistakes, enjoy making an effort and to keep on learning! Help children to understand that making mistakes is a vital part of learning something new – that everyone makes mistakes all the time and that they should be openly acknowledged so all can benefit. Helping others manage their mistakes is also important to encourage feelings of empathy and instances of active kindness.

We should try and pause before we 'swoop and sort' because mostly they can manage perfectly OK with the right support. Always try and praise the process of learning and not just the end result – so ensure that the 'how' and the 'what' of any activity are as important to the children as their completed art work on the wall – their cakes on a plate – or brilliant bike-riding!

Keep in mind that praising staff for just being "worth it" can be negative and damaging.

We need to provide children with lots of opportunities for open-ended physical play with a wide variety of interesting loose parts to engage with and explore. This will give them many energising moments to make mistakes – work out what went wrong – how to do it differently next time – what extra help may be needed or what resources may be better. Let's adopt a more open and curious mindset in our relationships with children so we can fully appreciate the range of learning opportunities embedded in our activities.

Remember that resilience in children can be very situation specific. Some children are very resilient physically but not so much emotionally and can really struggle to cope with making mistakes in their work, group activities or if friendships change suddenly. Let's be careful about our responses. Sometimes we can be a bit quick to judge and label the staff member and the child as 'drama queens' because of their emotional responses.

Celebrate small victories often. A child conquers their fear of cycling unaided, a staff member picks up a slug, a parent passes her driving test. Stop , breathe and enjoy.

Resilience is often best supported when we are engaged in a community project, campaign or event. Whether visiting a local elderly group, contributing to a food bank, helping with the local community garden or supporting the bike charity, getting involved in an activity that is bigger than you can help develop resilience and the better management of adversity.

Understand how you can be useful in so many different ways. Open up your mind and think of your role as one where you are constantly' recycling, upcycling and repurposing' yourself and your colleagues so you can be 'braver than you believe – stronger than you seem – smarter than you think – and twice as beautiful as you ever imagined.'!

Remember that resilience is not just for surviving the worst day of your life, it's for thriving every day of your life.

And - Success is not the key to happiness, happiness is the key to success if you love what you're doing you will be successful
Albert Schweitze

Bitesize help

Read: We need to talk about money by Otegha Uwagba

Read: Repotting your Life by Frances Edmonds – Elliot and Thompson Ltd 2021

Read: This too shall pass' – Julia Samuel – Penguin 2021

Watch: March of the Penguins

Listen: Gloria Gaynor I will survive

Check Out : www.amightygirl.com and www.able-futures.co.uk

Resources: Early Years Staff Wellbeing: A Resource for Managers and Teams (July 2021) Dr. Erica Douglas-Osborne, Dr Rachel Lyons, Amit Nelinger & Tim Linehan www.annafreud.org NCFE CACHE Level 2 Certificate in Understanding Mental Health in the Early Years

Open University BOC: Supporting Young Children's Mental Health and Wellbeing

Thoughts for today, and every day!

I can get through this – I will get through this – I will survive – I will be stronger – this too shall pass.

Start a journal

Journaling just means setting aside a little quiet, undistracted time to sit down and think about your life. It may include writing down a record of what happened that day, offloading about something that is really bothering you or noting something that has inspired you.

Notes

Notes

Further reading

50 Fantastic Ideas for Sustainability

Teach children to reduce, reuse, recycle, repair and be respectful with 50 fun activities for encouraging environmental sustainability.

By June O'Sullivan and Nick Corlett

The Early Years Movement Handbook

A Principles Based Approach to Supporting Young Children's Physical Development, Health and Wellbeing

By Lala Manners

The A to Z of Early Years

Born from questions raised on her early years blog, June O'Sullivan brings a combination of advice, good humour and plain speaking to address themes that come up time and time again.

By June O'Sullivan

Leadership Skills in the Early Years: Making a Difference

Provides ideas and suggestions to address the issues facing leaders, enabling leadership into a future where we can all help make a big difference.

By June O'Sullivan

June O'Sullivan Blog
leyf.org.uk/junes-blog

THINK FEEL DO 9798403821131

First published in Great Britain by London Early Years Foundation

This edition published 2022

www.leyf.org.uk

London Early Years Foundation is a charitable social enterprise Reg. Company 2228978 Reg. Charity 299686

A CIP catalogue record for this book is available from the British Library.

Printed by Kindle Direct Publishing.

Printed in Great Britain
by Amazon